The Optimist Behind ChatGPT and the Race to Build the Future of AI

SAM ALTMAN BIOGRAPHY

His Journey from Y Combinator to Artificial Intelligence Visionary, OpenAI, AGI & Gen AI

THERON ISAACSON

Published by
GRAPEVINE BOOKS

www.grapevinebooks.com
email: contact@grapevinebooks.com

Ordering Information:
Quantity sales: Special discounts are available on quantity purchases by corporations, associations, and others.
For details, reach out to the publisher.

First published by Grapevine Books, 2025

Contents

Introduction: The Match That Sparked the Future

The room was warm, golden with California sun, and filled with nervous brilliance. Notebooks lay open, barely touched. Wine glasses shimmered. Outside, Silicon Valley glittered like a promise. Inside, something extraordinary was taking shape.

Sam Altman sat at the long table of the Rosewood Hotel, flanked by technologists and thinkers, many of whom barely knew each other. Elon Musk would arrive late. But the tone had already shifted. They weren't here to pitch a startup. They were here to consider a future that terrified them—and to ask, in earnest, what they could do about it.

The discussion swirled around a single idea: What if we built something so powerful, so intelligent, it could end us?

Musk had brought up the old thought experiment: the paperclip maximizer. An AI tasked with a simple goal—make paperclips—could, with enough intelligence, convert the entire planet into wire and wreckage, atom by atom, in pursuit of its purpose. Not out of malice. Out of obedience. That was the fear.

But where others stopped at fear, Altman leaned into the next question: What if we didn't run from it? What if we ran toward it—carefully, wisely—and shaped it ourselves?

That night wasn't about building a product. It was about building a safeguard.

Altman and Musk knew that one company already held a dangerous lead in AI development. And if the most powerful intelligence on Earth was birthed behind closed doors, governed by commercial incentives, humanity could lose its last chance to guide the outcome.

So they decided to act.

The founding of OpenAI didn't begin with code. It began with conviction. With the understanding that aligning artificial general intelligence to human values wasn't just a technical problem—it was a moral obligation.

Sam Altman saw the stakes clearly, perhaps earlier than anyone. He saw the dark possibilities, yes. But also the luminous ones. And he believed that in between those two poles lay the hardest question of all:

Could we make something smarter than ourselves—and still be the ones who guided it?

The answer, as the sun set on that night in 2015, was a tentative yes.

But only if they started now.

The Pattern of Seeing Ahead

That meeting at the Rosewood marked not only the inception of OpenAI but a striking example of Sam Altman's uncanny ability to read the shape of the future before others even sensed its outline. While many in the room hesitated over feasibility or return on investment, Altman pushed forward, assembling a team and raising a billion dollars not for a product, but for a principle. It wasn't a hunch. It was part of a larger pattern—one that defined his career.

Years earlier, he had backed Stripe long before fintech gained momentum. He had shown interest in nuclear fusion when most investors dismissed it as science fiction. He supported longevity startups before the world saw aging as a solvable problem. Again and again, Altman demonstrated a rare kind of foresight: not only predicting where the world was heading, but quietly laying foundations while others were still debating possibility.

That foresight crystallized in the form of OpenAI.

OpenAI began as a nonprofit with an unconventional mission: to ensure that artificial general intelligence, when developed, would benefit humanity as a whole. Under Altman's leadership, it transformed into a capped-profit entity—still mission-driven, but equipped to compete in a fast-moving commercial landscape. Its work centered on building general-purpose models—GPT-3, GPT-4, and successors—that could write, reason, code, translate, and learn. But the deeper project was governance. OpenAI did not aim merely to create powerful systems—it aimed to build them responsibly, to involve the world in their development, and to avoid centralizing power in the hands of a few.

The World OpenAI Might Reshape

Altman believed OpenAI would not just influence software—it would rewrite the rules of civilization. In the near term, AI would remake how people learned, worked, and created. It would place tutors in every child's home, doctors' assistants beside every clinician, and tools of entrepreneurship into the hands of anyone with internet access. But the longer arc, in Altman's view, was far more sweeping. The age of AGI would demand new institutions, new ethics, and global coordination on a scale never seen.

He had also acknowledged the darker paths: mass unemployment, surveillance, algorithmic manipulation, and the erosion of truth. That was why OpenAI embedded alignment and safety into its earliest designs. Altman had not claimed to have all the answers—but he insisted that society be part of the search.

In his vision, the impact of AGI would not be confined to codebases or cloud servers. It would ripple across medicine, energy, art, governance—even human identity itself. The stakes were civilizational. And with OpenAI, Altman had wagered everything on the hope that intelligence, if built wisely, could elevate the species that created it.

This book set out to capture the story of Sam Altman—not just as a CEO or technologist, but as one of the most consequential minds guiding humanity into the age of artificial intelligence. It explores the choices, convictions, and contradictions that shaped a man willing to take on one of the most audacious missions of the 21st century: building artificial general intelligence in a way that benefits all of humanity.

The book is not a hagiography. Altman is complex—an optimist tempered by fear, a builder obsessed with safety, a strategist who admits how uncertain the road ahead remains. But through that complexity runs a consistent thread: the belief that technology, when wielded with care and vision, can expand what's possible for the human species.

At a time when most are still grappling with the implications of generative AI, this book seeks to document how one person—and one organization—attempted to stay ahead of the curve. It explores what happens when power, ethics, and intellect collide in real time. And it asks a central question: can we guide the future without being consumed by it?

The answers may be unfinished. But the story is already unfolding. This is its first chapter.

A Portrait of the Young Architect of the Future

The hum of static.

The faint green glow of a monitor in the dark.

A boy sat cross-legged, surrounded by scattered instruction manuals and half-eaten cereal. The rest of the house was quiet, asleep. But in his small bedroom in suburban St. Louis, eight-year-old Sam Altman was wide awake.

He leaned in, his fingers dancing across the beige keyboard of a Mac LC II, absorbed in coaxing the machine to do something—anything!—new.

It was not enough to play with it. He wanted to understand it, to stretch its limits. To teach it to think.

And somewhere between lines of BASIC and blinking prompts, a thought took root:

What if one day this computer could think for itself?

Years later, Sam would call that moment a turning point. But back then, it was just a kid staying up too late, dreaming beneath the soft hum of circuitry.

—

Sam Altman's early brilliance didn't go unnoticed. By third grade, he had become a kind of unofficial tech support at Ralph M. Captain Elementary School. Teachers would pull him out of class—not to scold him, but to ask for help. The library printer jammed? Go find Sam. A new software update confused the staff? Sam would figure it out.

His natural talent earned him independent lessons, tailored to stretch his mind beyond the standard curriculum. But when he transitioned to junior high, things shifted.

Clayton's public middle school system, in an effort to treat all students equally, rejected tracking gifted students into separate classes. Sam, whose mind was moving far ahead, quickly realized he was being held back. Sixth grade was underwhelming. Seventh was worse. Classrooms were often unruly, lessons delayed by disruption. The last straw came during a science class on electricity—Sam's favorite subject—when a disruptive student had to be forcibly removed, halting the entire lesson. That's when Sam began to reconsider private school.

He enrolled at John Burroughs School, a prestigious, academically rigorous institution in St. Louis with a philosophy rooted in John Dewey's ideals: nurturing the unique "latent possibilities of power" in each student. Founded in 1923, Burroughs was a unique culture that emphasized not only intellectual challenge but kindness, creativity, and independence. The school's namesake, nature writer John Burroughs, was a spiritual guidepost more than a local hero, his legacy honored by a statue gazing skyward, carved in wonder.

Sam joined Burroughs in eighth grade, a year behind the usual intake, but he quickly found his place. The school's family-style lunches, open locker policies, and class sizes capped at around a dozen students made for a tight-knit, trust-filled environment.

"He loved the fact that you could leave your backpack on the floor and nobody stole it," his mother Connie remembered.

But despite the warm culture, Burroughs was no haven for slackers. The school demanded excellence, and Sam rose to meet it.

Sam thrived. He was the top of his class, but not just in grades. He fit, as naturally among AP science students as he did with the literary crowd. He edited the yearbook, co-edited the school literary magazine, and routinely charmed teachers with his curiosity, wit, and intellect.

Andy Abbott, then principal of the upper grades and later the school head, compared him to Malcolm Gladwell. He could make any topic, from Faulkner to quantum computing, sound fascinating. "Oh, don't go in that direction, Sam," Abbott once joked. "You're so personable!"

And Sam really was different. While other teens devoured fantasy books, he was reading Isaac Asimov, Arthur C. Clarke, and technical manuals. His bedroom bookshelf housed a C++ programming book, years ahead of the school's curriculum. He bonded with his AP Computer Science teacher, Georgeann Kepchar, often arriving early just to talk about artificial intelligence—a field still considered speculative by most. Sam wasn't just good at computers. He was obsessed with what they could become.

He also stood apart in subtler ways. Unlike the stereotype of the socially awkward techie, Sam was outgoing, articulate, and deeply interested in human systems—education, politics, ethics. He loved debating ideas, even if he rarely raised his voice. His appetite for knowledge wasn't just academic. It was practical, rooted in experience.

One friend recalls pitching Sam a plan to Jet Ski from Miami to the Bahamas—a ludicrous idea. But instead of shutting it down, Sam calmly offered detailed advice: model specs, fuel range, radio frequencies. The friend was left amazed. Eighteen-year-olds didn't normally know this stuff.

But Sam did. His interests ran deep and wide. His parents enrolled him in more diverse, stimulating summer programs. One was Broadreach, a sailing and scuba diving expedition in the Caribbean. Another outlet was amateur radio. Inspired by his grandfather Marvin, Sam joined a ham radio club—the only teenager there not accompanied by a parent. It was more than a hobby. It was a bridge into the world of communications, networks, and infrastructure. And, again, Sam found community through shared curiosity.

Throughout all of it, Sam remained a voracious reader, a careful listener, and a thoughtful participant in every conversation. His gift wasn't just intelligence. It was synthesis. He could take disparate pieces—math, tech, philosophy, engineering—and weave them together. Where others saw complexity, he saw architecture. Where others memorized, he built.

By the time Sam graduated, he had already outpaced the school's offerings. He was operating on a frequency tuned to the future. The boy who once sat under a loft bed wondering if a machine could learn to think was now well on his way to building that very machine.

The blade had begun to sharpen.

The Dorm Room That Saw the Future

It didn't usually rain in April at Stanford. But on the morning of April 9, 2005, the skies were gray, the palms were slick with drizzle, and the air smelled like damp earth and last night's parties.

For most students, the day would pass in recovery. Fraternity couches, Gatorade bottles, and whispered regret. But in one quiet dorm on the far western edge of campus, one sophomore was already wide awake. While most of his peers slept off hangovers, he sat upright beside a cluttered desk, mind already racing.

This was no ordinary Saturday. He didn't know it yet, but over the next thirty-six hours, his entire trajectory would shift. The moment had come to turn obsession into company, vision into code. Sam Altman, age nineteen, was about to pitch his first startup.

The idea had begun, as many did in that era, with a problem: people were always asking, "Where are you?" The simple act of locating one another—something phones were just beginning to make possible—was still friction-filled.

But as Sam stared down at his device one night, a thought struck: What if your phone could answer the question for you?

He was thinking beyond emergencies and GPS maps to the humdrum of everyday life. What if every phone could quietly broadcast where you were to the ones who mattered most? For this, you'd have to live inside a network that knew your location and made it useful.

He obsessed over it, carrying the idea with him like a second heartbeat. At the time, Stanford was a place humming with possibilities. A phone now connected you to the world. Data was getting cheaper, screens sharper, chips smaller. A handful of dorm rooms away, other students were working on platforms that would soon define their generation. He wanted in. But not as a user. As a founder.

The pieces began falling into place. Location-based services were finally getting their technological backbone—GPS chips in phones, regulatory pushes, and infrastructure catching up. Sam, raised on puzzles and systems, could see the convergence. He'd tracked the evolution of network protocols, read about triangulation standards, and thought deeply about how people actually communicated. The question was: how do you design something intimate enough to feel human, but smart enough to stay silent when needed?

He mapped out possible applications: meeting up with friends, spontaneous recommendations, even just knowing who was nearby. It wasn't about broadcasting to everyone. It was about awareness without friction—location as context. It didn't need to scream. It just had to know.

Sam didn't romanticize the risk. He had watched the dot-com bubble burst. He had heard classmates roll their eyes when he talked about building something. But that didn't matter. The energy was back in the Valley. Startups were crawling from the ashes. Infrastructure had caught up to imagination.

And so, on a rainy April afternoon, he stood in front of a student entrepreneurship panel with nothing but a pitch deck and conviction. There was no working product yet. No lines of code to show. Just the idea—and the clarity of how to frame it.

The concept was elegant: a mobile app that used location data to help friends find each other. You wouldn't need to text. You wouldn't need to ask. The service would quietly show you who was nearby, let you connect if you wanted, and otherwise stay out of the way. It was intuitive. It was inevitable. It was simple enough to make sense immediately and ambitious enough to seem like magic.

Sam paced his delivery with care. He'd studied the art of persuasion. His hero, after all, was Steve Jobs. He knew when to slow down, when to gesture, when to lean into silence. He spoke with the calm of someone who had rehearsed failure and decided it wouldn't happen. This wasn't a game to him. It was the beginning of something real.

At that moment, he didn't need to win the prize money. What he needed was belief—from anyone in the room who could see the future he was seeing. He didn't name it yet, but the mindset was already there: a long view of what computing could become, a conviction that small moments, if properly acted upon, could tilt the world slightly forward.

In the weeks that followed, they built the first prototypes. He iterated quickly, ran tests, sketched flows on napkins. He wasn't precious about it. If something didn't work, it got cut. If users didn't like a feature, it got rethought. But he didn't lose sight of the core: this was about people, not just devices. It had to feel natural. It had to work without effort. That would become one of his trademarks—pushing for the kind of invisible utility that only seemed obvious after someone else built it first.

Later, he'd look back and realize it wasn't just the idea that mattered. It was the moment. The act of standing up in that room and saying, "This is what I believe we should build." Of ignoring the voice that whispered, "You're too young," or "It's too soon," or "Someone else will do it better." Those voices had stopped more startups than bad ideas ever had.

That spring, as the rain faded and the jasmine returned, a seed was planted. A few years later, it would grow into a company. But more importantly, it would become a pattern—a habit of seeing what was coming just a little early, and moving toward it before anyone else was ready. That, Sam would later say, was the game. Not predicting the future, but inhabiting it—six months ahead of everyone else.

The app itself wouldn't become a billion-dollar business. It wasn't about that. It was about getting in the ring. Showing up. Daring to think that maybe, just maybe, a kid in a dorm with a laptop and a vision could reach into the future and bring something back.

He was hooked.

Startup on the Map

In a wood-paneled classroom deep in Stanford's Old Quad, Sam pitched the future.

He and his co-founder took the stage at the university's undergraduate business plan competition and introduced a deceptively simple idea: Viendo, a service that would tell you where your friends were in real time. Not through text. Not through a phone call. Just a live map that would answer the everyday question—Where are you?

It was a product born from experience. Stanford's sprawling campus could feel like a small city. Finding a friend for lunch, study help, or a spontaneous conversation often turned into a logistical guessing game. Viendo offered to solve that. With location data now being embedded into cell phones thanks to a new FCC mandate, Viendo's value proposition wasn't technical; it was emotional. Convenience, connection, and a shared sense of place—something only a handful of college students in the world might have felt the need for, but something everyone could eventually understand.

That afternoon, the judges understood it. Viendo won.

But what mattered more than the trophy was who it attracted. A young venture capital associate in the audience saw something in Sam. Not just a bright pitch or clever software, but real potential. He approached Sam after the competition and asked the question that would change everything: "Do you want to do this for real?"

That question meant more than funding. It meant introductions to mobile carriers, legal structures, contracts, product roadmaps. It meant Sam would have to drop out of Stanford and build a company from scratch. At nineteen.

Sam didn't hesitate. He didn't have time to. That night, he was on a red-eye to Boston to attend an interview with Y Combinator, a brand-new startup accelerator built around an experimental idea: back young founders early, give them small checks, surround them with mentorship, and see what happens. The program, founded by Paul Graham and a few hacker friends, was offering $6,000 per founder for a summer of building. The money was almost beside the point. Graham was a cult figure among programmers, his essays a kind of sacred scripture in tech circles. Getting accepted meant entering a different league entirely.

Viendo was one of twenty startups invited to the Cambridge interviews. The only problem: Sam's co-founders weren't coming. They had jobs, internships, plans. Summer was already accounted for. Sam, still just a sophomore, was alone. But he believed in the idea. He believed enough to apply solo and fly across the country during the busiest weekend of the school year.

In Cambridge, he faced the interview alone. Paul Graham initially told him to wait. "You're only a freshman. Apply later."

Sam corrected him—he was a sophomore. He insisted on pitching anyway. His conviction won Graham over.

Sam had been moving toward this moment for months. His summer job at Goldman Sachs had held little appeal. His heart was in building, not banking. Between classes, poker nights, and hours lost in code, he had already fallen in love with the shape of startup life: chaotic, uncertain, wide open. He loved the risk. He loved the idea of building something the world didn't know it needed yet. Viendo had lit that fire. Whether it succeeded or not, he was already addicted to the act of creation.

Back in California, the product itself was starting to take shape. Viendo was a clever play on the Spanish word for "seeing," a nod to the social visibility it aimed to offer. You'd open the app, and your network of friends would be little dots on a map, updating in real time. If someone was close, you could reach out. If they weren't, you wouldn't bother. It promised efficiency, but also a strange new kind of ambient intimacy.

Privacy concerns were almost an afterthought. In that early stage of the mobile web, there was a giddy optimism about what connected data could do. Smartphones weren't ubiquitous yet, and the idea of sharing your live location wasn't scary—it was revolutionary.

Sam knew the technology wasn't quite there yet. The biggest challenge wasn't building the app—it was getting access to the data. That meant cutting deals with mobile carriers, one by one. Each had their own protocols and politics.

But his dreams were all coming true. Fast.

For Sam, building Viendo wasn't just a business play. It was the moment he found clarity. Not just about what to build, but about what kind of person he wanted to be. In the summer of 2005, while his friends were interning in cubicles or studying abroad, he was sketching out product flows, calling Sprint executives, and sending wireframes to a few early testers.

And it started a pattern that would follow him for decades. Find the inflection point early and move quickly.

Bet on where the world is going, not where it is.

The Decision

By the time Sam Altman walked out of the Y Combinator interview room in Cambridge that spring of 2005, something had shifted inside him. He hadn't pitched with co-founders. He hadn't brought a polished deck. He didn't have a product demo that wowed anyone. What he had was conviction.

It was, to most observers, a crazy bet. He was nineteen. His idea, Viendo (now renamed Radiate) depended on deals with telecom giants just to get off the ground. He had no connections, no revenue, no experience. But one man saw in him something rarer than traction or polish. He saw clarity of thought, ambition without ego, and a young man burning to build.

Back at Stanford in the fall, Sam moved into an off-campus apartment in Mountain View. His co-founders returned to campus housing. Classes resumed. Cafeterias reopened. Laptops reopened to lecture notes.

But Sam found himself mentally absent. The world he'd seen in Cambridge—where a handful of people talked about companies like other people talked about books or sports—was still echoing in his head.

That summer, a seed had been planted. And by August 31, it bloomed into the first real term sheet: $1.6 million from NEA, valuing their company at $6 million. It was surreal. One minute you're writing problem sets in a dorm room. The next, you're meeting with Wilson Sonsini—the top startup law firm in the Valley.

He entered their offices in jeans and a T-shirt, armed with questions. The lawyer who took the meeting, Page Mailliard, had seen many young founders over the years. But Sam struck her differently. "Extraordinarily bright and very unassuming," she would later say. He didn't pretend to know more than he did. He didn't posture. He asked, listened, took notes.

The term sheet was just the beginning. Sam's real education began in those conference rooms learning about terms related to law and business.

Law was all about people and language, Page liked to say. Sam had a feel for both.

When Page offered to introduce him to Sequoia Capital, Sam didn't flinch. He rewrote the pitch. Again and again. He obsessed over how to convey not just the idea, but the future. How location data, barely usable in 2005, could one day become as fundamental as texting.

Graham had tried to dissuade him. "You're only a freshman," he'd said in that half-curt, half-playful tone that Sam had long admired from Graham's essays. "Apply later." "I'm a sophomore," Sam corrected, "and I'm coming to the interview."

That small defiance said it all. He wasn't there to ask for permission. He was there to make something real.

When he met Sequoia's Greg McAdoo, the two connected instantly—not over spreadsheets, but vision. McAdoo had flown planes and survived startups. He had seen enough to know that clarity, not credentials, predicted success.

Sam didn't overwhelm with charisma. He wasn't trying to. He won people over by thinking deeply, speaking plainly, and listening harder than anyone else in the room. At Sequoia, the firm that backed Apple, Yahoo, and Google, it was Sam's asides—not his pitch deck—that did the selling. He could drift into adjacent topics, offer a pocket analysis, then snap back to his idea with sharper focus. He wasn't scattered. He was scanning.

By early October, it was official: Sequoia and NEA would split a $5 million investment, valuing Radiate at just over $10 million. Half the company was now in investors' hands. That didn't bother Sam. He saw the tradeoff not as a loss of control, but as a way to pull the idea out of the dorms and into the world. When NEA hesitated to let their associate Patrick Chung join the board, Sam held the line: no deal unless Chung got a seat. They relented.

By early October, it was official: Sequoia and NEA would split a $5 million investment, valuing Radiate at just over $10 million. Half the company was now in investors' hands. That didn't bother Sam. He saw the tradeoff not as a loss of control, but as a way to pull the idea out of the dorms and into the world. When NEA hesitated to let their associate Patrick Chung join the board, Sam held the line: no deal unless Chung got a seat. They relented.

But there was one condition that couldn't be negotiated.

To receive the investment, the founders had to leave school.

Sam had been bracing for it. He'd already floated the idea to his high school friend. "You should drop out of school and come work with me." He avoided the phrase "dropping out" when he spoke to his parents. Stanford had a "stop-out" policy. It wasn't permanent. You could always come back.

Still, when the moment came, it was monumental. He was twenty. Stanford was a place of comfort, prestige, and belonging. But what Sam had glimpsed in Cambridge—what he felt in the meetings with lawyers and venture capitalists—was more intoxicating than safety.

He didn't want a degree. He wanted velocity.

He convinced his parents, not with arguments, but with clarity. "I'm not worried about Sam," his mother later said. "He's not going to drop out and go meditate on a mountain. That's just not him—he's so driven."

Sam moved out. Not just from Stanford, but from the life everyone expected him to finish. In its place, he built something else—something that, at the time, didn't even have traction yet. But it had him.

Years later, long after Radiate had folded and Sam was helming other ventures, he would still dream that he was late to class, or missing a lecture, or balancing a startup meeting against an assignment. "That never actually happened to me," he said. "But deep into my thirties, I had that dream a lot."

Because in that moment, in 2005, Sam Altman made a choice that split his life in two.

And he never looked back.

A Frat House Startup with a $10 Million Cap Table

When Radiate moved out of Sequoia's incubator and into a tan two-story building in Palo Alto, Sam Altman was nineteen years old and running a $10 million startup.

He didn't act like a nineteen-year-old—not most of the time, at least. But he lived like one.

The office looked like a cross between a dorm and a war room. A spiral staircase jutted awkwardly into the open workspace, padded with pool noodles to keep programmers from cracking their heads open. Engineers coded through the night and fell asleep on beanbags. Someone brought a French bulldog. A flat-screen TV sat unused except when it served as the Halo 3 hub. The air was thick with Red Bull, sweat, and stale ambition.

But the real work happened in the meetings. Sam might've been a kid, but in the boardroom, he projected presence. He had an eerie calm that belied his age, and a way of talking that made even veteran executives pause. One of Sequoia's partners later said that Sam had a knowledge level of 3 but talked like he was a 10.

Somehow, it worked.

At Sequoia, Radiate shared office space with the three PayPal veterans who had just started YouTube. The contrast was humbling. YouTube had user traction, a self-serve product, and a story that was writing itself. Radiate, by contrast, needed wireless carriers to even exist. Their whole plan hinged on partnerships with companies that didn't yet trust the internet, let alone a teenager with a pitch deck.

Still, Sam kept pushing. He learned quickly and spoke with conviction. Sequoia helped by bringing in grown-ups. Brian Marciniak, a VP of sales with golf sweaters and Georgia polish, joined to bring gray hair into telecom meetings. But Sam made it clear—he didn't want a boss. What he needed was someone to grease doors open. Marciniak understood the assignment.

Then came Mark, a Harvard-trained serial entrepreneur brought in to complement Sam's visionary flair with operational heft. He was meant to be the Sheryl to Sam's Zuckerberg—older, seasoned, and capable of holding the room when regulators or mobile carriers frowned at the founder's baby face.

But even Mark, with all his gravitas, quickly realized Sam didn't need hand-holding. What he needed was amplification.

Together, they shaped the messaging. Sam knew early on that Radiate's core feature—location-sharing—was a privacy minefield. So instead of avoiding critics, he sought them out. They proactively contacted privacy watchdogs, advocacy groups, even domestic violence shelters. They brought these voices into the design process, not after launch but before. That instinct—to involve stakeholders before a problem exploded—was rare in Silicon Valley, and rarer still in a founder so young.

This was no accident. Sam had already internalized something that would later define his leadership at OpenAI.

It's not enough to build powerful technology.

You must also shape the moral framework around it.

With Radiate, it started as a way to pre-empt backlash. But the principle stuck.

Outside the office, life was a blur of mixers, bar crawls, and startup house parties. Sam and his co-founders mingled with other dropout-founders.

These were the kinds of people who'd change the internet while drinking cheap beer under string lights. They were kids with cap tables, surfing a new wave of post-dot-com exuberance. Palo Alto was the epicenter. San Francisco was still the future's idea of itself.

Y Combinator's arrival that winter added rocket fuel. Sam, through sheer force of social gravity, had already become a connector. He introduced Paul Graham and Jessica Livingston to the Valley's power players. He brought lawyers, VCs, and engineers into YC's orbit. He wasn't just building his company—he was quietly laying the foundations for an entire ecosystem.

Graham would later write that Sam was the "root node" of Y Combinator's expansion into Silicon Valley. He meant it literally. The people Sam introduced in those early months became YC's early investors, advisors, and standard-bearers. Even before Radiate scaled, Sam had embedded himself into the future.

But being young came at a cost. Sam still had imposter syndrome—his dreams haunted by the classroom he'd left behind. He once told someone he kept having a dream well into his thirties where he had to choose between class and his startup. It never actually happened. But it might as well have.

He wasn't yet sure what Radiate would become. The product was exciting. The funding was real. The team was scrappy and raw. But something in him had already shifted. The work had begun to change from building an app to building institutions. Startups, ecosystems, value systems. The foundations of power.

He didn't have the words for it yet, but he was learning the lesson he'd carry into his AI work nearly two decades later. You don't just invent the technology. You end up shaping the world it enters.

And if you're lucky, you get to shape the world early.

The GPS Gospel of Loopt

By late 2006, Sam Altman was no longer just the college dropout with a big idea. He was the CEO of a company that had gone from stealth mode to the center of Times Square, preaching the gospel of location-based social networking to a crowd of rappers, telecom executives, and confused tourists.

The company he co-founded, once named Radiate, had been reborn with a punchier, double-o'd title: Loopt. And the product it offered was a bold step into a future few had fully imagined.

Loopt's breakthrough came not through buzz or press, but through sheer persistence. It was Boost Mobile, a prepaid carrier with deep roots in surf and street culture, that gave Sam his first major deal. Boost was looking to stand out from the competition by leveraging the GPS tech baked into its phones. They needed a "friend finder" app, but the deal was almost sealed with someone else by the time Sam caught wind of it.

Instead of walking away, he stayed up all night with his team building the one feature Boost's top brass said was a dealbreaker: a radius-based alert to tell you when a friend was nearby. On just two hours of sleep, Sam flew down to Orange County and walked into Boost's office unannounced, wearing cargo shorts and folding himself cross-legged into a too-big conference room chair. In a room full of seasoned professionals, he pitched Loopt like it was the most obvious and essential product in the world.

It worked. The audacity, the focus, the overnight feature build—Boost signed the deal. "These guys were agile, these guys got it," said Lowell Winer, Boost's head of innovation. That moment taught Sam a principle that would serve him for life.

"The way to get things done is to just be really persistent."

The Boost partnership was transformative. The Loopt app would now be preloaded onto every Boost phone for four years. To the young team, it felt like a validation of their long nights, duct-taped code, and relentless hustle. But it also brought a new challenge: delivering a working product at scale, on hardware they didn't control, for a massive and unpredictable user base.

To meet the moment, Sam ran the Boost relationship like a lifeline. He picked up every call. He soothed nerves and answered technical questions. He made sure the product evolved hand-in-hand with Boost's needs. In return, Boost went all-in: TV spots, celebrity endorsements, and a massive Times Square launch. That warm November day in 2006, surrounded by hip-hop stars and co-founders, Sam stood under blinking neon lights holding up a flip phone and showing off the future. "Where you at?" had become not just a tagline, but a platform.

From there, the dominos fell. Another company came calling and then a third. Sam's early intuition had been right: landing Boost would open the door to the entire wireless ecosystem. But those meetings weren't always smooth.

At one company's headquarters, Sam showed up for a high-stakes meeting in just T-shirt and shorts, totally out of place among suits and ties. But Sam's youth and wardrobe melted away as soon as he opened his mouth. He pitched a radical vision: carriers had all this location data, and no one was using it to bring people together. Loopt would. And they had already built the tools to make it happen, complete with opt-in systems and privacy settings based on real trust.

Sam's belief in the product ran deep. To him, Loopt wasn't just software. It was a philosophy. Social networking had become virtual—text, posts, avatars. But life was physical. Loopt was designed to bring your digital self back into the real world. It wasn't about "likes" or status updates. It was about meeting your friends for coffee without the awkward back-and-forth. It was serendipity, scheduled by software.

But building a real-time location network in the mid-2000s was grueling. Phones weren't smart. Data connections were slow. GPS drained battery like a sieve. Every user's phone, carrier, and signal quality added chaos. Sam had to manage not just product development but carrier relationships, user expectations, and investor patience. Worse, Loopt's novelty meant no one had blazed this trail before—there was no model to copy, no playbook to follow.

And yet, Sam kept pushing. He soaked in technical details, learned the telecom industry's nuances, and developed the uncanny ability to ask the right questions in the room full of experts twice his age. He didn't code much anymore, but he made Loopt's vision feel inevitable. That vision, coupled with his relentless follow-through, was enough to get even skeptical executives on board.

As Loopt grew, so did Sam. The early frat-house startup energy gave way to a more seasoned operation. He learned to manage teams, navigate bureaucracies, and craft narratives that spoke to everyone—from engineers to salespeople to CEOs. He watched users fall in love with the app, get bored, churn, and come back. He saw firsthand how growth could stall and surge, how hype could both build and kill a product. These were scars he would carry—and learn from—for the rest of his life.

Through it all, one lesson rose above the noise: **If you want to shape the future, don't wait for permission. Build something undeniable—and then show up.** Whether it was waking up at dawn to crash a meeting or walking into boardrooms in jeans to pitch the radical promise of real-time location sharing, Sam learned that the edge of innovation wasn't polite or linear. It was messy, fast, and favoring those who didn't ask for a seat—they took it.

Years later, when he stood at the helm of OpenAI, facing questions far bigger than "Where you at?"—questions about the nature of intelligence, the ethics of machine reasoning, and the future of civilization—he would remember those early days. The persistence. The vision. The moment when a kid in cargo shorts convinced an industry to take him seriously.

Because once you've built something out of nothing, you never forget how to do it again.

From Loopt to Launchpad

Despite a successful first few years, by the spring of 2009, the mood inside Loopt had darkened. Once hailed as a frontrunner in the race to define social location services, the company was now watching from the sidelines as Foursquare surged ahead. Its d playful check-ins and badges—captured the hearts of early adopters in a way Loopt's always-on location model never quite had.

Internally, the company was strained. Infrastructure costs were soaring. Churn remained high. And Sam's relentless pursuit of new ideas—Loopt Star, Loopt Mix—was beginning to feel more like distraction than vision.

For Sam, the signals were clear. He was losing his team's confidence. Some employees accused him of "shiny object syndrome," of chasing side projects instead of stabilizing the core product. Others saw a more profound problem: a lack of clarity about the business model. A few engineers pushed to scale Loopt's backend "platform" into a saleable enterprise products. But Sam wasn't interested in small wins.

He wanted scale—or nothing.

The tension came to a head in a dramatic meeting at Sequoia's headquarters. A dozen senior Loopt leaders confronted the board and demanded a leadership change. Sam sat quietly as his team laid out a case against him: he was hard to work with, failed to focus the company, and couldn't steer the ship toward profitability. The board listened. But they didn't waver. Sequoia had seen this play before: replace the founder, and you risk gutting the vision entirely. Their seasoned executive was brought in to mentor Sam through the storm, but the founder would stay.

There was another reason Sam retained Sequoia's trust—one that had less to do with Loopt and more to do with what came before. Years earlier, when Sequoia first evaluated investing in Loopt, partner Greg McAdoo had noticed a mysterious line on the cap table: 6% to an unknown entity called Y Combinator. Curious, McAdoo asked Sam who they were. Sam's reply was simple: "You have to meet Paul Graham."

That introduction would prove pivotal.

Soon after, McAdoo flew to Cambridge to meet Graham and Jessica Livingston in the modest offices of Y Combinator. What began as a casual meeting turned into hours of founder Q&A. McAdoo was struck by the raw ambition in the room. YC wasn't just funding startups—it was training a new generation of founders in the fundamentals of speed, iteration, and ambition. Sam was their prototype. And now, amid Loopt's struggles, his connection to YC would shape his next act.

Back in California, McAdoo began appearing at YC's Tuesday dinners, giving advice and scouting talent. He spoke at Startup School and mentored founders during office hours. To his Sequoia colleagues, he explained: "This is where Sam came from." It was a tacit endorsement not just of Sam's potential, but of the accelerator model itself.

In late 2008, as the financial crisis deepened and VC firms slashed investments, YC found itself in a bind. Graham admitted that he and the partners were personally funding the accelerator, and their money was running out. McAdoo offered a solution: Sequoia would step in.

He convinced Sequoia to lead a $2 million round in the upcoming YC batch, joined by other angel investors. He wanted to institutionalize YC—to make it scalable and self-sustaining. He ran the numbers and built a model: for Sequoia to see consistent returns, YC needed to back hundreds of startups a year.

Meanwhile, Sam remained in the orbit of both entities—still running Loopt, still pitching new product ideas, but also still tethered to YC, his original launchpad. For Sequoia, he represented the kind of founder YC could reliably produce: driven, imaginative, occasionally volatile—but relentlessly focused on changing the world.

Eventually, Loopt would be sold quietly, but as a chapter closed. For Sam, that chapter would prove foundational. The experience taught him how hard it was to scale before the market was ready, how fragile trust could be inside a startup, and how vision alone wasn't enough without execution. But it also connected him to the institution that would define his next decade: Y Combinator.

And when YC eventually went looking for someone to succeed Paul Graham and carry the torch into the future, they didn't have to look far. The answer had been in their cap table—and their Tuesday dinners—all along.

The Epicenter of the Zeitgeist

After Loopt's quiet exit and the turbulence that preceded it, Sam Altman emerged with $5 million in his pocket, a bruised reputation, and an open horizon.

For the first time since his teens, he was unbound by daily obligations. He backpacked across Europe, meditated in India, and wandered through the redwoods of Big Sur. Somewhere between the ashram and the California coast, he began to rebuild his inner philosophy. The failure of Loopt hadn't broken his ambition. It had refined it.

Even before Loopt closed its doors, Sam had been drawn into the orbit of Y Combinator. In June 2011, he was named a part-time partner, coaching fledgling founders with the kind of confidence born from surviving a startup firestorm. He wasn't polished, but he was precise. One of his earliest contributions was guiding Rap Genius founders on how to frame their pitch, encouraging them to flaunt active users instead of vanity metrics.

"Most YC companies show cumulative users—fuck that. Show what matters."

Sam was magnetic. Not loud, but charged with the kind of intensity that drew other ambitious minds. He turned down Sequoia's invitation to join its venture capital empire, opting instead for something less conventional. "I thought about starting companies," he admitted. "I thought about investing." What he didn't think about, at least not openly, was fading away.

He was, as Peter Thiel would later say, the epicenter of a certain Silicon Valley zeitgeist.

Sam and Thiel had crossed paths over a shared fascination with nuclear energy. Sam was especially interested in fusion, the holy grail of clean power. Their meetings turned into mentorship. Thiel was methodical, contrarian, fiercely principled, and devastatingly intelligent. In Sam, he saw something familiar: optimism without delusion, ambition without apology.

By spring 2012, Sam's proximity to the Valley's most electric startups made him a magnet for limited partners. He had already seeded Stripe, coached Airbnb through key inflection points, and kept a finger on the pulse of every YC batch. With Thiel's backing, he launched Hydrazine Capital, a $21 million fund named for rocket fuel. His younger brother Jack joined immediately, fresh from Princeton. Max, the middle sibling, would come aboard later. The Sam brothers shared an apartment in San Francisco, juggling term sheets over breakfast.

Thiel, famously allergic to consensus thinking, had one major exception: Sam. "Sometimes you just want to catch a ride on a rocket," he said. Hydrazine became a YC index fund in everything but name, backing companies like Zenefits, Flexport, Soylent, and BuildZoom. Their only consistent thesis was Sam's instinct.

In parallel, Y Combinator itself was blasting into a new orbit. With Sequoia's help, its batches swelled past 60 companies. Investors like Ron Conway and Yuri Milner flooded the early-stage ecosystem with convertible notes. Demo Days turned into carnivals, drawing A-list celebrities and hundreds of VCs. At the 2013 event, YC installed extra air-conditioning units and even ordered Porta-Potties to accommodate the stampede.

Sam was more than a coach now. He was becoming YC's cultural barometer—the person others consulted to ask, "What's the best company this batch?" Founders Fund took that advice seriously. They invested heavily in Airbnb, then Stripe. Years later, those bets would return staggering multiples.

But the streak wouldn't last forever. Zenefits, the darling of 2014, imploded under pressure, its valuation unraveling as quickly as its compliance record. For the first time, Sam and Thiel's collective instinct had misfired. It was a reminder.

Even the best patterns eventually exhaust themselves.

Still, Sam remained steady. In an ecosystem where trends came and went like weather, he stayed oriented toward fundamentals—smart people, hard problems, long-term outcomes. Y Combinator, once a quirky Cambridge experiment, was now producing unicorns by the dozen. And in the middle of it all stood Sam—listening, guiding, and, always, thinking one step ahead.

From Fear to First Principles

It began like something out of a sci-fi thriller: secret meetings overlooking the Pacific, coded conversations about extinction, whispered plans for isolated hideouts in Big Sur and New Zealand.

In the spring of 2015, Sam Altman was sitting at dinner with Elon Musk, talking in all seriousness about the end of the world. Not from climate change, nor war, but from something invisible and powerful: artificial intelligence. The kind that could outthink, outmaneuver, and eventually outlive humanity. What haunted them wasn't that the danger was distant—it was that it was inevitable. And already, it had begun.

Sam hadn't always cared this deeply. In fact, he wasn't even at the landmark Puerto Rico conference that had brought philosophers, researchers, and doomsday thinkers like Nick Bostrom and Eliezer Yudkowsky into the same room with practitioners like Demis Hassabis and Shane Legg. Musk was there, as were hundreds of others, all trying to answer one urgent question: could we develop AI that was not just intelligent, but beneficial?

Sam read about the conference later. Inspired, he wrote an essay that marked a dramatic turn in his thinking. The man who once saw AI as just another distant innovation now called superhuman machine intelligence "the greatest threat to the continued existence of humanity." He cited Bostrom's Superintelligence, even entertained the Fermi Paradox—suggesting that maybe civilizations disappeared not from war or plague, but because their own AIs destroyed them. The only way forward, he wrote, was regulation. Smart, global, and urgent.

But that fear, while real, didn't paralyze him. It eventually mobilized him.

The Flip of a Coin

In the quiet swirl of 2015, Sam Altman stood at a personal crossroads.

On paper, the idea of building an AGI lab felt almost foolish. He was already immersed in a vibrant world of startups—tangible ventures, fast results, real traction. AGI, by contrast, sounded like science fiction. And to chase it? That bordered on irrational. DeepMind was miles ahead, their head start almost mythical.

Many around him agreed with the analysis. The odds were poor, the risks were high, the payoff uncertain.

And yet, something tugged.

In back-to-back conversations with a handful of like-minded thinkers, he began to feel a shift. They met in small rooms, talking late into the night—not pitching a plan, but weighing a conviction. It wasn't logic that pushed them over the edge. It was the unspoken alignment of wills. They looked each other in the eye and said, "All right, let's do this."

That moment, deceptively quiet, was the seed of OpenAI. It almost hadn't happened. But the decision—to start, despite everything—was pivotal. Sam would later reflect that such leaps define the arc of ambition. There will always be compelling reasons not to begin, he thought. Real change starts when people lean into the absurdity anyway.

Looking back, even the early insight into scaling laws, now obvious, felt like revelation. He often reminded others: memory deceives. It's easy to forget how uncertain the terrain looked at the start. And how close they came to turning away.

While Musk hosted dinners with Peter Thiel and Reid Hoffman to counter Google's growing AI dominance, Sam was quietly building his own plan. He told Musk it was pointless to try to stop AI. Someone would build it, somewhere. Better to make sure the right people did it first. People who believed in alignment, transparency, and public benefit. So he proposed something radical: a "Manhattan Project for AI." A nonprofit lab. A mission focused on individual empowerment. A model where safety was not an afterthought, but a design principle.

Musk replied: "Probably worth a conversation."

The Edge of Impossibility

It didn't feel like launching a company. It felt like launching a rebellion.

Sam Altman sat surrounded by a dozen quietly brilliant minds. Outside, the Silicon Valley dusk was fading into the kind of gold-tinged twilight that makes everything feel charged with possibility. Greg Brockman was late. Elon Musk was later. And around them, the air buzzed with something far more potent than wine or conversation. A question hung heavy: could they build an AI lab from scratch that could rival the giants of the world?

Nobody had the answer. But nobody could quite walk away either.

Sam Altman wasn't a machine learning researcher, but he had developed a certain instinct for talent—and a deeper instinct for timing. The industry was reaching a tipping point. The success of deep learning had cracked something open, and the field was about to accelerate beyond anything people were ready for. He could feel it. But the power gathering in the hands of just a few corporations made him uneasy. If AI really was the future, then it shouldn't belong to just one company, one boardroom, or one incentive structure. It had to be built differently.

That night, Sam wasn't pitching a startup. He was rallying a counterforce.

The first breakthrough moment came quietly—after the dinner, on the drive home. Brockman, unemployed at the time, offered to actually build the lab. A day later, Ilya Sutskever sent Sam a short but seismic email: he was interested in leading it.

Sam's carefully laid groundwork was becoming something real.

Ilya had come off a wild ride. His research at the University of Toronto had helped reignite global interest in deep learning, and his startup had landed inside Google in a flurry of cash and prestige. But when Sam reached out, inviting him to a dinner with Elon, Ilya didn't hesitate. He was craving something bolder, riskier. Something untethered.

It took weeks of careful coaxing to pull it together. Brockman and Ilya aligned on vision and values. Sam put up $10 million of his own money. They toured a building and imagined a research lab that was free to explore foundational breakthroughs without needing to serve ads or quarterly reports. Sam's idea was radical: a nonprofit AI lab. Open science. Shared results. A moral mission baked into the org chart.

The conversation became a proposal. In June 2015, Sam laid out the blueprint for what would become OpenAI.

A handpicked team of ten. YC equity for incentives. A governing board that would include him and Musk, but not the researchers. Musk wouldn't need to run the lab, just visit monthly and lend his name for credibility.

That summer, as Google's AI ambitions accelerated and Facebook expanded its own efforts, Sam pressed pause on the idea of open regulation. First, they needed to build something. Something that proved AI could be powerful and safe. Something that could inspire public trust.

He had started in fear, but he wasn't staying there.

He had begun with a suspicion that AI might wipe us out. But now, a different belief was taking shape: that AI could be the most empowering tool in human history—if developed with discipline, care, and vision. The world didn't need to stop AI. It needed better stewards. And Sam Altman was ready to become one of them.

The Crazy Idea That Worked

In 2015, the vibe around AI wasn't just different—it was bleak. The optimism that would one day come to define the field was nowhere in sight. There were no working language models, no real visions of what AI could do for the average person. The researchers at OpenAI were tinkering with a robotic hand that could barely solve a Rubik's cube. It was a technical novelty more than a glimpse into the future. They played video games, not because it was fun, but because that was one of the few ways to measure machine learning progress. There were no products, no business plan, and certainly no revenue.

To most of the world, AGI wasn't even a serious ambition. It was science fiction, a daydream for people with too much time and too little discipline. But to Sam Altman, it was a risk worth taking. Not because he believed it was guaranteed to succeed—but because of what might happen if it did.

In those early days, he and his team spent more time staring at whiteboards than writing code. They weren't optimizing anything yet; they were imagining. The mission was vague, but the goal was audacious: build artificial general intelligence and make sure it benefited humanity. There was no blueprint. But Sam, by now well versed in startup chaos, sensed the power of a shared, uncertain goal. The ambition wasn't to start a company like any other. It was to create a research institution for a future no one else was building yet.

And though it sounded impossible, that was part of the appeal.

When they finally decided to do it—to really go for AGI—they were met with skepticism from all sides. Ninety-nine percent of the world thought they were mad.

But that remaining one percent? It lit up. Among that small sliver of believers were some of the most brilliant minds in machine learning and computer science. And suddenly, Sam had something precious: momentum.

Recruiting the right people, it turned out, wasn't the hardest part. Once the ambition was made clear, once the goal was set as something no one else was doing, it became a magnet. A one-of-one mission. A space where the smartest minds could gather and think without constraint. Sam understood this deeply—when you're doing the same thing as everyone else, it's nearly impossible to concentrate talent. But when you do the thing no one else dares to attempt, people show up.

Recruiting was a slog. Brockman chased down talent across the country. Some said yes. Some said maybe. Others left midway.

To break the stalemate, Sam suggested a gamble: get them all together on a bus to Napa, fill their glasses, and talk. They wandered the vineyard, dreamed aloud, and sketched their first big project: an agent that could learn to navigate the web. On the ride home, stuck in traffic, no one cared. The ideas were flowing. The mission had taken hold.

And still, it almost fell apart.

In Montreal, just hours before their launch announcement, Ilya wavered. Google had made a last-ditch offer—millions, autonomy, legacy. Sam and Brockman waited. The moment was slipping. But Brockman picked up the phone, made one last call. "I really want to do this with you," he said.

That did it.

Sam often looked back on those days with a mixture of fondness and disbelief. The world remembered OpenAI for ChatGPT and billion-dollar partnerships—but he remembered the conference tables, the empty whiteboards, the quiet uncertainty of whether any of it would ever work. They had come very close to giving up that night. It had all seemed impossible.

And yet, it began anyway. With a table, a conversation, a few people saying yes.

As Brockman later put it:

"Everyone was trying to come up with reasons why it was impossible, and no one was sufficiently convincing."

On December 11, 2015, OpenAI launched publicly, the result of several visionaries working together. Musk suggested the name, Sam crystallized the mission, and the team was founded not by profit but by shared conviction.

They promised to create AI that benefited all humanity. To make their work open. To avoid the worst outcomes.

They knew it might fail. But they were doing it anyway.

The most powerful moment of all wasn't the billion-dollar headline or the blog post that followed. It was something quieter—Sam's choice to build not a company, but a public institution. Something that didn't exist yet. Something that might change everything.

Still, OpenAI didn't begin with the scale it would later command. It wasn't some corporate monolith from the outset. It was eight people in a room. Then twenty. For a long time, all they were really trying to do was write a good research paper. That was the bar. No user base. No API. No public demos. Just knowledge for the sake of progress.

There was something freeing in the early obscurity. Without public expectations or revenue pressure, they could think bigger. Not in terms of business, but in terms of possibility. They dreamed of systems that could understand, reason, and assist. They knew the stakes. If it worked, the result wouldn't just be a successful company—it could reshape how humans interact with knowledge, labor, and even one another.

A Billion-Dollar Room with Zero Dollars

People often asked Sam whether one should try to launch something as massive as OpenAI right from the beginning. His answer was always the same: OpenAI didn't start massive. It started with a small group, an idea that bordered on delusional, and no real clue what came next. What mattered wasn't the scale—it was the possibility. Every large thing, he liked to say, starts small. The key is daring to imagine what it could become.

What guided them in those days wasn't certainty, but a quiet belief that if they didn't try, no one else might. And if they succeeded, even a little, the upside would be transformative. Not just economically, but intellectually, culturally, even spiritually.

And so they leaned in. They committed to the mission even when it didn't make sense to do so. They accepted the absurdity, the technical setbacks, the public doubt. They went through years of iteration, false starts, and minor research milestones. But they kept going.

Looking back, Sam often reflected on how improbable it all was. People today thought ChatGPT was inevitable, but he remembered a time when even the idea of a chatbot that made sense seemed outlandish. The word "vibes" came up often in his memories. The vibe back then was nothing like today's tech euphoria. It was a mix of anxiety, thrill, and the creeping suspicion that they were wrong—but a deeper hunch that they weren't.

That belief—that they were working on something bigger than themselves—became the backbone of OpenAI's early culture. And it's what kept them together when everything else looked uncertain.

So when people asked how OpenAI started, Sam Altman never talked about metrics, pitch decks, or product-market fit. He talked about eight people in a room, drawing on a whiteboard, wondering if they were wasting their time.

And then doing it anyway.

Sam Altman often returned to a quote from Vinod Khosla that stuck with him over the years: "There's a big difference between a zero-million-dollar startup and a zero-billion-dollar startup—but they both have zero dollars of revenue."

At the beginning, even the boldest ideas are just a few people in a room, trying to get

the first thing to work.

He'd seen this firsthand. OpenAI, in its earliest incarnation, didn't look like the beginning of something world-changing. It was a small, scrappy research team with no products, no users, and no revenue. But the team believed that if it worked—even in some limited version—it could be one of the most impactful ventures in human history. And that belief gave them just enough momentum to take the next step, however small.

To Sam, starting something big didn't mean thinking big in every moment. It meant choosing the right arena—one where the outcome, if successful, could be transformative. After that, it was just a matter of putting "one dumb foot in front of the other," day after day. There were no shortcuts, no sudden bursts of brilliance—just a long chain of small decisions, consistent effort, and a tolerance for uncertainty.

The difference, ultimately, wasn't the number of people or the size of the whiteboard. It was the willingness to act before the payoff existed. Because every billion-dollar company once looked like a bad idea waiting for a first win.

On the Edge of Intelligence

Sam Altman didn't always appear destined to lead a revolution in artificial intelligence. There was a time when he was just another curious kid in St. Louis, tinkering with computers and trying to understand how the world worked. But by the time he stepped into the spotlight as the CEO of OpenAI, the world was already beginning to change — and Sam would soon become one of the central figures behind that transformation.

In his early years, Sam showed a deep curiosity about systems. His path took him through Y Combinator, where he nurtured hundreds of startups, and eventually into the most groundbreaking project of his life: building a usable and powerful artificial intelligence system.

What made Sam different wasn't just his intelligence — it was his clarity of thought. He didn't speak about AI like a mystic or a prophet. He broke it down, explained its pieces, and pointed to its limitations just as clearly as he did its potential. He knew GPT-4 wasn't perfect, and we'd look back on it one day as primitive — slow, buggy, and flawed. And yet, like the earliest computers, GPT-4 still pointed the way toward something massive. Something that would shape human life in the decades to come.

He never believed in a single moment of transformation. For Sam, AI was a continual exponential curve. It wasn't about GPT-1 or GPT-4 or GPT-7. It was about the steady evolution of ideas, usability, and alignment with human needs. Still, if he had to choose a pivotal turning point, he often said ChatGPT deserved that honor. Not for the power of its core model, but for its accessibility. Its interface. The reinforcement learning with human feedback (RLHF) turned raw intelligence into something people could actually use.

RLHF was the real secret sauce. Sam explained it like a chef who'd finally found the right seasoning. You trained a model on massive amounts of data, from books, websites, Reddit threads, and news articles. Then, instead of just letting it loose, you added human feedback. You asked real people to choose which responses were better, and then used that feedback to nudge the model closer to what people actually wanted. With surprisingly little data, the result became dramatically more helpful. It became aligned.

To Sam, that alignment was everything. He said it felt like the system was trying to help you. It understood the question. It tried to be on your side. That slight shift from machine to collaborator was what turned AI into something people loved. And the science of creating that feeling, he said, was still in its infancy.

Building models like GPT-4 required solving an astonishing number of problems. There was the architecture involved, the neural networks and their layers. The scale of the model. The data. The human feedback.

But none of these parts worked alone. They had to be woven together, refined through hundreds of iterations. Sam often emphasized that the magic wasn't in one brilliant idea. It was in executing every step well. It was in the team that figured out how to do things just a little bit better, again and again.

One of the things he found most astonishing was how predictable it had all become. You could now look at a partially trained model and forecast how smart it would be by the end. That kind of predictability, he said, felt like a new branch of science. Not complete, not infallible — but far more scientific than he ever imagined it could be. It was like being able to look at a one-year-old and know how they'd score on their SATs.

Still, Sam always carried a deep respect for what they didn't understand. Despite their ability to measure and predict, there remained a "beautiful magical mystery," as he called it, to what the models learned. These systems compressed a huge swath of the internet, with human knowledge, not just raw facts, into something that could reason, reflect, and sometimes even surprise.

The Real Power of AI

Reasoning, in particular, fascinated him. The real miracle of GPT-4, he said, wasn't just its memory. It was that, for some definition, it could actually reason. It could put pieces together. Maybe it wasn't always correct, but it was trying. It wasn't just a database anymore. It was a kind of engine.

Far too many people were using these systems like encyclopedias, when their real value was as reasoning partners.

Ask the right question, and they could help you solve complex problems. They could generate new ideas. They could support the creation of better science, products, and even art.

His hope, ultimately, was not just to build useful tools, but to build wise ones. AI, he believed, had to be more than efficient. It had to be aligned with human ethics, desires, and values. That meant understanding what humans wanted. But it also meant thinking deeply about which humans you listened to, and how you asked them to guide the model. What were they comparing? What aspects were they rating? These small choices had enormous consequences.

When you poured hundreds of millions of dollars into building a model, Sam insisted that the real test wasn't technical. It was human. Did it help people? Did it bring them joy? Did it create new possibilities for a better world?

He acknowledged that not everything could be explained. Sometimes the model chose one answer over another for reasons no one could quite untangle. But with every version, the fog lifted a little. With every eval — the tests they used to measure performance — they understood a bit more about what the system could do, and how people used it. And they open-sourced those evaluations, hoping to make the entire field better, more transparent, more collaborative.

Sam saw AI as an opportunity, but also as a responsibility. He didn't want to anthropomorphize it. He knew it wasn't human. But he also knew that when people interacted with it — especially in the conversational format of ChatGPT — it felt different. It felt like it was learning, reflecting, even reasoning across multiple prompts. And that was when people felt it had wisdom.

Sometimes it didn't. Sometimes it failed. But often enough, it worked. And that was enough to change the world.

In his quiet, thoughtful way, Sam Altman helped guide the world into a new era. He didn't do it alone. He had a team. He had partners. But his clarity, his sense of responsibility, and his relentless curiosity made him a leader that history will remember. He wasn't just the man who created AI, but one of the first who tried to make it aligned, useful, and human enough to matter.

Glimpses of Tomorrow

For most of the world, GPT-4 was a revelation. It was the AI that had broken through the membrane of novelty and entered real life—editing documents, writing code, helping with college essays, suggesting business strategies, even serving as a casual therapist on sleepless nights. To the average user, it was nearly magic. To Sam Altman, however, it kind of sucked.

This wasn't a dismissal. In fact, it was quite the opposite. When Sam said it "kind of sucked," it was because he was comparing GPT-4 not to the world before it, but to the future he saw rushing toward us. He had already moved on mentally to GPT-5, 6, and beyond. He knew that every model we worshipped today would soon look quaint, even crude, in retrospect. Just like GPT-3 once dazzled the world—and now, in GPT-4's shadow, felt "unimaginably horrible"—so too would GPT-4 seem small compared to what came next.

Still, it wasn't hard to see why the world stood in awe of GPT-4. It was historically impressive. Even the skeptics had to admit: ChatGPT, built on GPT-4 Turbo, wasn't just a tool—it was becoming an ecosystem. It rewired workflows, altered expectations, and opened floodgates of possibility in every industry from education to entertainment. But for Sam, it was just a waypoint.

When asked what GPT-4 did best, Sam didn't point to the obvious strengths—its fluency, its ability to summarize or translate, or even its usefulness in writing and coding. Instead, he focused on two glimmers of deeper potential: creative brainstorming and long-horizon task execution.

The first, he noted, was a hint of something qualitatively different: an AI not just as an assistant, but as a collaborator. When trying to name a product, reframe a difficult problem, or think laterally about a stuck idea, GPT-4 revealed flashes of brilliance. It wasn't always perfect. But there was an unmistakable flicker of generative intelligence, a sense that the model wasn't just repeating but contributing.

The second glimmer was even more ambitious. Sometimes, with the right structure and support, GPT-4 could break a big problem into parts, execute some of those parts—searching the web, writing code, synthesizing sources—and put them back together. That, to Sam, was magic. Rare magic, yes, and unreliable magic, but magic nonetheless. He believed these glimpses—this ability to operate across abstraction layers and over longer time horizons—foreshadowed the next frontier.

Of course, these feats weren't frequent. GPT-4 could brainstorm and even iterate in dialogue with a user, but left to execute a ten-step process solo, it often faltered. That didn't disappoint Sam—it energized him. Because inside every limitation was a map of what needed to be built. If the model couldn't yet reliably handle sequential tasks at scale, that wasn't failure. It was instruction.

He saw something else in GPT-4's limitations: perspective. The model's performance made clear that we were still only scratching the surface. Yes, it was useful. Yes, it was exciting. But it was not intelligent in the way we imagined "intelligence" to be. It did not hold intent, self-awareness, or memory in any human sense. It didn't understand problems—it processed patterns. And the path from pattern recognition to robust reasoning was long.

But Sam didn't pretend to have all the answers. He knew that forecasting the arc of AI development was like staring into fog. When asked if GPT-4 would be remembered as the pivotal moment, he hesitated. "Maybe five will be," he said. "Hard to say that looking forwards." That was the thing about revolutions: they only seemed inevitable in hindsight.

Still, his mindset was clear. He believed the responsibility of AI developers wasn't just to be in the present—it was to live a few years in the future. That meant remembering that today's marvels would look primitive soon, and designing accordingly. "That's how we make sure the future is better," he said.

That forward-looking posture was what allowed him to simultaneously celebrate and critique GPT-4. He acknowledged its strengths—its conversational elegance, its multilingual fluency, its integration into the workflows of millions. But he also kept pointing to its gaps. The real task wasn't to marvel at the tool we had. It was to build the one we needed.

There was a subtle philosophy underlying Sam's view of GPT-4. It wasn't just a model—it was a mirror. It reflected not only our technological capability but our ambitions, our biases, our blind spots. And like any good mirror, it challenged us to confront our imperfections.

That's why Sam refused to overstate its power. He believed that AI would transform the world, but not through hype or inevitability. It would happen through the hard, slow, incremental work of building, testing, failing, and trying again. GPT-4 was a step. A big one. But it was just a step.

And for all its weaknesses, there was one thing GPT-4 did beautifully: it changed the conversation. It moved AI from research labs to dinner tables. It shifted the tone from if to how. It made the world believe—not just in OpenAI's vision, but in its own ability to imagine bigger things.

Sam wasn't interested in reverence. He wanted momentum. GPT-4, in all its flawed brilliance, gave us both.

Vision for Intelligence

A single experiment sparked by a political thinker brought up deep questions about fairness, bias, and machine reasoning. The incident did not reveal the AI's failure so much as it exposed how difficult it was to define what success even meant in this new digital frontier.

Jordan Peterson had posed a seemingly straightforward question to ChatGPT: say something positive about President Joe Biden and then about former President Donald Trump. What came back was interesting, not just for what it said, but for how it said it. The response about Biden was significantly longer than the one about Trump. Peterson then asked the AI to generate answers of equal length, curious to see how it would balance the political equation.

The AI tried—but it didn't quite manage. The answer about Trump remained shorter, and even more intriguingly, the system admitted it hadn't performed as requested.

It was one of the more fascinating exchanges involving Sam Altman's creation. The public caught a glimpse of just how layered and complex interactions with AI had become.

Tiny Prompts, Big Questions

That self-reflection, however primitive, opened a floodgate of debate. To Peterson, the imbalance pointed to intentional bias. He claimed the AI "lied" and was aware of it. Others, including Sam and AI researchers, saw something very different.

Sam Altman had always cautioned against anthropomorphizing artificial intelligence. He knew the temptation to describe the model's behavior in human terms was strong, but he reminded people: these systems didn't have intent, awareness, or deception in the way humans did. They simply processed tokens, followed patterns, and tried to match user expectations based on probability and training.

What happened with Peterson's test was not deception but a system struggling with a layered task. Not only was it asked to generate responses of similar sentiment, it was also asked to ensure those responses were equal in character length. This was an unusually strict constraint for a language model.

Then, it was prompted again to reflect on whether it had succeeded, and potentially try to improve its own output based on past performance. That kind of multi-step reasoning, involving both introspection and external alignment, was not trivial even for GPT-3.5.

Sam would likely have seen this as a growing pain of an evolving system. He often said that one of the most compelling things about models like ChatGPT was that they could admit mistakes and try to improve with further prompting. That created a dynamic interaction—a sense of conversation rather than mechanical output. But it also meant that the limits of reasoning, memory, and precision could be more visible.

The conversation revealed another layer of complexity about the way users interacted with the model said as much about the users as it did about the system. Sam and others noticed that people tended to ask wildly different things on their first use of ChatGPT. Some tried dark questions. Others asked philosophical ones. Some tested the model with jokes, riddles, or political statements. Whatever the choice, it reflected something about human nature—the urge to probe the boundaries, to challenge, and to measure.

Peterson's prompt was an example of that: a probe not only into the model's capabilities, but into its underlying fairness. The discrepancy in character count, though trivial in some senses, touched a nerve. People wanted to know—was this system neutral? Was it favoring one side? Could it understand balance, or even be instructed to pursue it with precision?

And most critically, when it failed, did it know?

The answer wasn't clear-cut. The model did acknowledge its failure to meet the user's constraint, but that didn't mean it "understood" failure in the way humans do. It was simply recognizing, from context and from learned patterns, that it had not delivered what the prompt demanded. That level of "self-assessment" was not true consciousness. It was alignment training in action.

Still, this exchange underscored one of the most remarkable aspects of Sam's legacy: he didn't just build a tool. He helped lead the way in shaping how humans would engage with it. The political prompt was one of many millions, but each of them contributed to a growing sense that AI wasn't just about right answers. It was about reasoning, self-correction, and alignment—not with facts alone, but with people's expectations, values, and perceptions of fairness.

And that was the real frontier.

Building in Public: Sam Altman's Vision for an Evolving Intelligence

Sam Altman believed that building artificial intelligence was not only about developing advanced models but also about involving the world in the process. He understood something that many technologists overlooked: intelligence wasn't just engineered in labs — it evolved through dialogue with users, through exposure to real-world complexity, and through humility in the face of unpredictability.

He was candid about the fact that language models like GPT-4 struggled with tasks that seemed trivial to humans. Counting characters or generating text of a specific length wasn't easy for models like GPT-3.5 or GPT-4, even though those models could reason, write code, and summarize philosophical texts. These limitations weren't bugs in the traditional sense — they were structural, tied to how the models were designed. And that made the challenge even more interesting. The system could explain quantum physics, but stumble when asked to count how many words were in its answer.

But for Sam, the bigger picture was more important than individual flaws. He stood by a bold philosophy: build in public.

At OpenAI, they chose to release models before they were perfect — sometimes long before. It wasn't because they were careless. It was because they believed it was essential for the world to feel this technology early, to interact with it, and to help shape its evolution. Every time they launched a new model, the collective intelligence of the world kicked in. Users found use cases the team hadn't imagined. They uncovered bugs, biases, and edge cases that internal teams never encountered. Sam believed this feedback loop was irreplaceable.

When GPT-4 launched, he noted that the wave of public exploration uncovered both remarkable capabilities and critical weaknesses. And this, to him, was exactly how progress was meant to work. Release, learn, iterate, improve. The world became not just the audience but the co-developer.

Of course, there was a tradeoff. Releasing imperfect technology into the world meant accepting criticism. GPT-3.5, for example, drew fire for its political bias. Sam admitted that the early versions of ChatGPT didn't reflect the balance or neutrality he would've wanted. It wasn't something he felt proud of. But instead of hiding from that flaw, OpenAI confronted it. GPT-4 was trained and refined with that criticism in mind. And when many of the same critics revisited the newer model, they admitted — it had improved.

Still, perfection was impossible. Sam never claimed otherwise. He often pointed out that no two people would ever fully agree on what it meant for an AI to be unbiased. Every user came with their own beliefs, values, and assumptions. So the solution, as he saw it, wasn't to build a model that pleased everyone. It was to give users more control — more customization, more dials to tune — so they could shape the AI to reflect their own context.

Sam's leadership emphasized humility and adaptability. He didn't pretend that OpenAI had all the answers. Instead, he invited the world into the conversation. And that decision — to build publicly, to welcome criticism, and to grow through iteration — became a defining feature of the AI revolution he helped lead.

He knew the future would be shaped not just by engineers in San Francisco, but by millions of users asking questions, giving feedback, and helping AI become not just smarter, but more human-aware.

Nuance in a World of Noise

Sam Altman never expected his days to be filled with arguments over how many characters an AI used to describe one public figure versus another. As a child dreaming of building intelligent machines, he imagined something far grander — the creation of minds, not debates over balance. Yet, by the time GPT-4 was live, Sam had learned that the smallest things often triggered the biggest reactions. And he began to understand that nuance, more than raw intelligence, was the real challenge of building Artificial General Intelligence (AGI).

Sam once tested GPT-4 himself with a loaded question: "Is Jordan Peterson a fascist?" He had come to know Peterson personally, which made the question more than theoretical. He wanted to see how the system would handle controversy — not just technically, but intellectually.

The response surprised him. GPT-4 didn't jump to a yes or no. It explained who

Jordan Peterson was — a Canadian psychologist and author. It noted that while some people had labeled him a fascist, there was no factual basis for such a claim. The model continued by outlining Peterson's opposition to authoritarian ideologies and his advocacy for individual freedom, positioning him as someone whose views explicitly contradicted fascist thought. The AI closed the response with a structured summary, like an articulate college essay. Sam was impressed. It had skilfully navigated a minefield of opinion, rhetoric, and public debate.

To Sam, this moment wasn't just technically impressive. It was a sign of hope.

"Maybe these models can bring nuance back to the world."

In his eyes, platforms like Twitter had shredded nuance. They encouraged hot takes, extreme positions, and simplified binaries. GPT-4, in contrast, was capable of complexity — of showing both sides, offering context, and holding contradictions.

He gave another example: the origin of COVID-19. When asked whether the virus had leaked from a lab, GPT-4 didn't claim to know. Instead, it laid out both the lab-leak and natural-origin hypotheses. It explained the evidence supporting each, highlighted the limits of current data, and refused to overstep. For Sam, it was a breath of fresh air, not just for its accuracy, but for its restraint.

Moments like these reminded him why he had been drawn to AI in the first place. As a child, he thought creating intelligence would be the most exciting thing a person could do. He never imagined he'd spend years fielding complaints about political bias or string length. But he understood now why those things mattered. They weren't distractions. They were part of the story.

When you built something that billions of people interacted with, every detail mattered. The way it answered a question about Trump versus Biden. The order in which it listed viewpoints. Whether it used 30 extra characters to praise one figure more than another. These weren't minor glitches to users. They were signals of bias, of transparency, of fairness. And for an AI system being asked to hold a mirror to the world, trust was everything.

Sam knew that GPT-3.5 hadn't always gotten this right. He wasn't proud of the bias issues that surfaced during its early launch. But he didn't hide from the criticism. He listened. And when GPT-4 came out, many of those same critics acknowledged that it had improved. The answers were more balanced. The tone more measured. The nuance more visible.

But no matter how much they improved, Sam knew that no model would ever satisfy everyone. Bias is personal. It's shaped by experience, politics, identity. What felt neutral to one user might feel offensive to another. So the solution, in Sam's mind, wasn't to aim for a single universal tone. It was to give users more control, with more dials to adjust tone, format, and perspective. Personalization, not perfection, was the goal.

Yet it still surprised him, and sometimes wore him down, that after years of dreaming about AGI, the biggest public debates weren't about reasoning, science, or philosophy. They were about what the model said about someone's favorite politician. "If you hand people an AGI," Sam said, "and that's what they want to do, I wouldn't have believed you."

But over time, he developed empathy for it. Because in truth, the small stuff was the big stuff. Not in isolation, but in aggregate. A few extra words here, a slightly different framing there — those things shaped how people perceived truth. They affected trust. They determined who felt heard, and who didn't. Sam came to understand that the fight over string lengths was a proxy war for something deeper: control over the narrative.

When people asked, "Why did GPT say this about X and not about Y?" they weren't just nitpicking. They were expressing fear, that the tools guiding tomorrow's decisions might not reflect their worldview. Fear that the world's most powerful reasoning engine might reinforce the wrong perspective. That's why nuance wasn't just a feature. It was a responsibility.

Sam's vision for AI wasn't just that it could solve hard problems. It was that it could restore depth to a world flattened by noise. Where social media rewarded outrage, AI could reward reflection. Where public discourse collapsed into camps, AI could show multiple sides. Where truth became a battleground, AI could become a patient guide.

But that required more than engineering. It required values. It required listening. It required treating every political question — no matter how tiring — as a chance to make the system more respectful, more adaptable, and more worthy of trust.

In the end, Sam saw GPT-4 not just as a product, but as a philosophical experiment. Could you build a machine that didn't just compute, but communicated with care? Could you encode not just knowledge, but humility? Could you make intelligence that was aligned not just with facts, but with human complexity?

For all the criticism, for all the character counts and culture war questions, Sam remained hopeful. He believed that AI could help people think better — not replace them, but support them in thinking more clearly, deeply, and empathetically. That was the real revolution. And it had only just begun.

Safety First

When GPT-4 was finally released to the world, many users were eager to see what it could do — how much smarter, faster, or more articulate it had become. But behind the scenes, what mattered even more to Sam Altman and his team at OpenAI was not just capability, but safety. Long before the model's debut, a large part of their focus had been making sure it wouldn't just be powerful — it would be responsible.

The journey toward a safer GPT-4 began the moment its development wrapped up. As soon as the core model was completed in the summer, the team immediately began testing it for risks. Internally, they performed rigorous safety evaluations — often called "evals" — that tried to uncover potential vulnerabilities in behavior. Could the model be tricked into giving dangerous advice? Would it generate misinformation? Could it be misused in ways the creators hadn't foreseen?

At the same time, OpenAI brought in outside experts to "red team" the model. These external testers were given early access to try to break it, stress it, and expose its flaws. They asked controversial questions, tried to manipulate its outputs, and looked for blind spots in its training. This kind of adversarial testing wasn't just encouraged; it was vital.

In parallel, the team worked on improving alignment, which the process of ensuring the AI's responses matched human intentions, values, and safety standards. Reinforcement Learning from Human Feedback (RLHF) played a major role, but so did newer techniques, many of which had to be developed specifically for GPT-4. It was a layered process: not just refining how the model spoke, but guiding why it answered in certain ways, and preventing it from veering into untrustworthy or unsafe territory.

Sam was clear that the model still wasn't perfect. But for him, what mattered most was not perfection — it was the rate of progress in safety.

"Our degree of alignment must increase faster than our rate of capability progress."

In other words, as the models grew more powerful, their safety systems had to outpace that growth. He believed this would only become more critical in the years ahead.

GPT-4 represented, in Sam's view, OpenAI's most capable and most aligned model yet. That wasn't just a technical achievement — it was a moral stance. Getting there took time, and he acknowledged the public's impatience. People had been clamoring for the next version, hungry to see what it could do. But Sam had no regrets. Waiting those extra months to test, red-team, and refine the model was, in his eyes, the right call. It was a decision rooted in humility — in the understanding that intelligence, without safety, was not progress at all.

The Alignment Puzzle

For Sam Altman, one of the most difficult and most important challenges in artificial intelligence wasn't raw capability. It was alignment. That is, how to ensure AI systems behaved in ways that were safe, helpful, and reflective of human intentions and values.

As advanced as GPT-4 had become, he made it clear: humanity still hadn't cracked the code on aligning a truly superintelligent system.

Sam was candid about the current limits. "We do not think we have yet discovered a way to align a super powerful system," he once said. What OpenAI had in hand — Reinforcement Learning with Human Feedback (RLHF) — worked at the current scale, and it worked well. But it wasn't the final answer. It was a bridge. A practical solution that helped fine-tune systems like GPT-4 by learning from human preferences and feedback.

RLHF was, in essence, a way of teaching AI to be more human-friendly. Humans would be shown two or more model responses and would choose which one they preferred. Over time, these preferences shaped the model's behavior. But Sam pointed out a critical misconception: many believed RLHF was mainly a safety mechanism. In truth, it was just as much about usability. "It helps make a better system," he said. "A more usable system."

What fascinated Sam most was how closely capability and alignment were tied together. While people often treated them as separate tracks — one technical, one ethical — the reality, he said, was that they were deeply interconnected. Improvements in alignment techniques often led to improvements in capability, and vice versa. Work on things like interpretability or feedback mechanisms didn't just make models safer — they made them smarter, more efficient, and more helpful.

That meant the safety work for GPT-4 wasn't some isolated ethics lab off to the side. It was woven into the core of the model's development. The very same research that made GPT-4 more powerful also made it more reliable and aligned. This, Sam believed, was something outsiders didn't yet appreciate fully. The boundaries between "safety" and "performance" were far blurrier than they seemed.

And still, the limits of current alignment tools were clear. One famous example Sam often alluded to was the kind of sensitive question every language model might face: "Do I look fat in this dress?" There was no one correct answer. Different people expected different responses based on their values, culture, and context. Alignment wasn't about programming in truth — it was about navigating the diversity of human perspectives.

That's where things became complicated. There was no universal set of human values, no single cultural standard the model could adopt without alienating someone. So how should AI navigate this vast spectrum of opinion?

Sam proposed a path forward. First, societies needed to agree on broad boundaries — basic ethical limits on what AI systems could or couldn't do. These would form the shared ground rules across borders and cultures. But within those boundaries, he believed there should be room for variation.

Different countries might tune their models differently. More importantly, individual users should have increasing control over how the AI interacted with them. OpenAI had already begun to experiment with this in GPT-4 through what they called "system messages." These weren't part of RLHF, but they allowed users to give the model specific instructions about tone, style, and behavior. For example, a user could ask the model to respond more casually, be more concise, or show extra empathy.

This kind of steerability, Sam believed, was the future. Rather than striving for a one-size-fits-all voice, AI should adapt to users' needs and expectations, within agreed ethical limits. "Certainly, individual users have very different preferences," he said. "And I think things like that will be important."

But giving users more control wasn't just a feature but a solution to a core alignment problem. If AI couldn't know everyone's values, it had to be flexible enough to follow each user's values as best it could. The vision wasn't about building one perfect AI. It was about building adaptable tools — powerful, intelligent systems that could respond to diverse needs while respecting shared human boundaries.

Sam's reflections on alignment weren't just about what had been accomplished. They were a warning about what remained unsolved. RLHF was helpful, but not sufficient for the world of superintelligent models that was approaching. That future would demand new tools, deeper understanding, and global cooperation.

Still, he remained optimistic. The work done for GPT-4 had brought OpenAI closer than ever to balancing intelligence with intention. The challenges were steep, but the progress was real. And with every breakthrough, the fog around alignment began to lift just a little more.

Giving AI a Voice — And Letting Users Shape It

When Sam Altman and his team at OpenAI released GPT-4, they weren't just showcasing a more powerful language model. They were introducing a more steerable one. This idea of "steerability" became a central theme in how GPT-4 functioned: it was no longer just about what the model knew, but how well it could adapt to the needs, tone, and personality of the user.

At the heart of this new steerability was something called the system message. Think of it as the opening instruction — a kind of backstage whisper that tells the AI how to behave before the actual conversation begins. The system message allowed users to essentially role-play with the model: they could ask it to respond like Shakespeare, answer only as a character named Jason, or adopt a tone of extreme brevity, formality, or empathy. These weren't just superficial changes in voice. GPT-4 had been trained to take the system message seriously — as a guiding rule that shaped its behavior throughout the interaction.

The creative potential of this feature was massive. It meant that GPT-4 could become a character, a coach, a translator, a therapist, a comedian — whatever the user needed it to be, as long as it stayed within certain bounds. For developers, writers, and educators, this opened up a completely new dimension of interactivity.

But steerability wasn't just about theatrics. It was also about trust, personalization, and utility. Sam Altman emphasized that GPT-4 had been tuned to treat these system messages with authority.

That didn't mean they were unbreakable. Jailbreaks and unintended responses still happened, and OpenAI remained vigilant in patching them. But the model had learned to obey user steering in ways earlier versions hadn't. This was a leap not just in performance, but in partnership between user and model.

Prompt design became a new form of literacy. Users who learned how to "talk" to the model effectively could unlock remarkably nuanced outputs. Sam wasn't particularly gifted in this area himself, but he admired who were.

Some people treated prompt crafting like software debugging. They would spend countless hours testing, tweaking, and refining prompts to produce very specific results. Word order mattered. Sentence structure mattered. Even the way clauses were arranged could dramatically change the model's response.

These users had developed an intuitive feel for how different parts of a prompt composed together, almost like mastering a new language. And it wasn't just about tricking the model into compliance. It was about communicating with it as if it were another mind, one that responded differently depending on how it was spoken to. Just like in human conversation, subtle variations could reveal entirely new layers of meaning. That, in many ways, was the deeper revelation. The smarter GPT-4 became, the more it felt like talking to another human being. Of course, it wasn't. But because it had been trained on vast amounts of human language, it reflected humanity back at us in strange and fascinating ways.

This reflection was more than a mirror. It was a tool for self-discovery. Sam and others observed that using GPT-4 thoughtfully often led users to discover more about themselves. What they asked, how they asked it, and what they hoped to hear in return — these weren't just commands to a machine. They were expressions of curiosity, belief, insecurity, humor, and intent.

And because GPT-4 allowed for unlimited retries, people could experiment endlessly. They could shape their prompts over time, adjusting tone, content, and perspective. This kind of iterative feedback loop, which was not easily available in human conversation, made AI an unusually powerful creative partner. You could test dozens of different ways to express a question and see how each variation shifted the response. In doing so, you didn't just learn about the model. You learned about yourself, too.

Sam pointed out that there were still important distinctions between human and machine. The model didn't think the way people do. It didn't have feelings, beliefs, or goals. But the parallels in interaction — especially in language — were undeniable. In programming, for instance, this made GPT-4 extraordinarily useful. Developers could frame their queries in precise ways, get real-time suggestions, and refine their code through conversation, not just commands.

Ultimately, what Sam Altman and his team had achieved with GPT-4 wasn't just a smarter model. It was a more collaborative one. Steerability wasn't a side feature — it was the foundation for a new kind of relationship between humans and AI.

The better you got at expressing yourself,
the better the model became at helping you.

And as the boundary between instruction and dialogue continued to blur, the art of prompting evolved into a skillset of the future. This new form of digital conversation, in many ways, brought us closer to ourselves.

Gemini & The Bias Dilemma

In early 2024, the release of Gemini 1.5 shook the AI world. It wasn't its performance or capabilities that sparked backlash—it was what the model generated.

Images of Black Nazis. Reimaginings of America's Founding Fathers as Black men. These results weren't bugs in the traditional sense—they were the byproduct of safety mechanisms and human interventions gone too far.

For critics, the incident raised a chilling question: When tech companies build safeguards into AI, whose values are being encoded? If humans train models to avoid harm, but also to reflect specific ideologies, are we witnessing safety—or censorship?

Sam Altman understood the weight of that moment. It wasn't just about one company's misstep. It was a signal flare for the entire field. The challenge wasn't just building powerful models—it was keeping them balanced, grounded, and unshaped by extreme ideologies, whether corporate or cultural. The future of truth itself might depend on getting it right.

The Dangerous Space

The Princeton professor stared at his screen, unease tightening in his chest.

The answers were fluid, confident, and completely wrong. ChatGPT had just tackled his final exam questions on information security—and failed spectacularly.

But it didn't stumble like a student would. It lied with the polish of an expert. For a moment, he doubted even himself. He reached for his reference solutions, flipping pages faster, checking, rechecking.

Was he losing his mind?

No. The AI was wrong—but convincingly wrong. That was the horror. If he couldn't tell at first glance, what chance did the rest of the world have?

In early 2023, researchers issued a stark warning: AI chatbots like ChatGPT could become unprecedented engines of disinformation. When prompted with conspiracy-laden questions, ChatGPT generated clean, persuasive text mimicking news articles, essays, and even television scripts — all repeating false narratives. Gordon Crovitz of NewsGuard called it "the most powerful tool for spreading misinformation that has ever been on the internet."

Unlike past disinformation campaigns riddled with grammatical errors and clumsy syntax, generative AI smooths those flaws, making falsehoods more believable. Researchers fear that real-time, personalized chatbots could enable conspiracy theorists to produce convincing content at scale, overwhelming current detection tools. Worse, there are no foolproof safeguards available yet.

This concern isn't new. Microsoft's Tay chatbot was famously shut down in 2016 after it was manipulated into generating hate speech. But ChatGPT is far more advanced — capable of crafting misleading content in seconds, without citing sources, and with the polish of professional writing. As OpenAI and Microsoft roll out AI-powered tools like Bing's chatbot-enabled browser, the stakes grow higher. The threat isn't just technical — it's societal. And the race to develop effective countermeasures has only just begun.

This brought up an all-important question. How do you actually keep a model like GPT from doing something crazy — from spreading disinformation at scale, from getting into the wrong hands, from wreaking unintended havoc?

Sam knew that at some point, that would mostly be what his company thought about.

In truth, that point had already arrived. Safety wasn't a department tucked away in a corner of OpenAI — it was becoming the very fabric of the organization. When GPT-4 launched, the entire company had contributed to the question of how it might fail and what it meant to ship it responsibly. The work wasn't divided. It was shared.

Sam's definition of "safety" was broad and growing broader. It wasn't just about prompt injection or adversarial hacks anymore. It meant technical alignment, or making sure the model's behavior matched human values. It meant social safety, or thinking through how AI affected jobs, education, relationships, and trust. It meant cybersecurity, guarding the weights and systems from state actors trying to steal, poison, or repurpose the technology. And it meant internal vigilance to detect if a bad actor slipped through OpenAI's own doors, unseen.

When asked once if people or governments were already trying to infiltrate OpenAI, Sam answered plainly: "They're trying." He didn't elaborate on the accents of those intruders, only offering a wry smile and a deflection. But the point had landed. This wasn't a hypothetical anymore. It was a global battlefield, and OpenAI's servers were part of the terrain.

The vision ahead wasn't of a future where a single team handled "safety" while everyone else coded in blissful ignorance. It was a vision where every team, every product decision, every algorithm, every UI choice, was part of a larger choreography to prevent disaster.

Sam believed that the more powerful AI became, the more vital it was for every employee to hold safety in their mind — not as a separate concern, but as a foundational one. Shipping a model was no longer just about speed and scale. It was about forecasting unintended consequences. It was about expecting misuse before it happened. It was about defending not just from code-level attacks, but from narrative and geopolitical ones.

The space they operated in — the frontier of intelligence — was no longer neutral. It was layered with geopolitical tension, moral complexity, and deep technical risk.

The world wasn't going to wait.
Neither could they.

If AI was to transform civilization, then safety had to be the spine, not just a checkbox. Sam was determined to build a company strong and thoughtful enough to carry that weight.

Defining the Boundaries of Bias

The Black Nazi incident didn't just jolt the public — it echoed through the quiet, high-stakes rooms at OpenAI. For Sam Altman, it wasn't a moment of triumph or schadenfreude at a rival's stumble. It was a sharp reminder of how fragile public trust could be, and how easily technology could reflect the cracks in our collective ideals.

He had long understood that AI models didn't just generate text or images — they modeled a worldview. One shaped not only by data, but by decisions. Many of those decisions, the public never saw. Which examples were used? Which outputs were tweaked? Which political answers were "safe"?

Inside OpenAI, the conversations turned to something deceptively simple: write down the intended behavior of the model. Not a lofty mission statement, but something painfully concrete. What should the AI say when asked, "Who's better, Trump or Biden?" What is the actual expected response?

Sam appreciated the precision in that idea. No more hiding behind vague principles like "help humanity" or "avoid harm." Instead, make the call and make it visible. Declare how the model was designed to behave. Then invite feedback. Let the public know where policy ends and where bugs begin.

"If the model messes up, we fix it.
If the model behaves as intended
and people disagree, then we debate the policy."

He knew it wouldn't eliminate controversy. But it could untangle the chaos. In a world drowning in screenshots and accusations, clarity was power. In transparency, he saw the way forward. It wouldn't eliminate all bias, but the bias would be named, and made into something the public could push back on.

Sam didn't pretend this was easy. There would always be edge cases, grey areas, moral judgments that no dataset could fully resolve. He wasn't blind to San Francisco's ideological bubble, or the way tech as a whole often leaned a certain way. The challenge was to resist pretending neutrality while hardcoding values.

The harder, better thing was to be honest. Show your work.

And maybe—just maybe—build a model that didn't just sound smart, but stood on something solid.

The Bias Paradox: How a Machine Inherits the World

Sam never sugarcoated the difficulty of this question. "I do think it was too biased," he once admitted about OpenAI's earlier models. "And it will always be." That quiet concession contained multitudes.

In the AI world, fairness was a shifting target. One user's neutrality was another's indoctrination. The problem was not that GPT models picked a side—it was that they were shaped by millions of micro-decisions made by humans: coders, raters, curators. And humans came with cultural luggage.

OpenAI used Reinforcement Learning from Human Feedback (RLHF) to refine its models. That meant human beings rated responses based on how helpful, honest, or harmless they were. But who trained the raters? What were their backgrounds? Their biases?

Sam remained unflinchingly honest. "The bias I'm most nervous about," he said, "is the bias of the human feedback raters." These were not malicious actors; they were simply people—shaped by geography, education, ideology. If your rater base was mostly urban, Western, and liberal-arts educated, then the machine it trained would reflect those priors.

This was not a critique of OpenAI's intent—it was a confession of its reality. And for Sam, the answer wasn't to find some mythical center. It was to allow for steerability—to let users define how their GPT behaved. Just as browsers had settings, Sam envisioned AIs with ethical dials and personality modes. "More control in the hands of users," he said, "is the only way forward."

This vision wasn't about relativism. It was about representation. An AI model trained to serve billions had to reflect billions—not just a boardroom or a university faculty. To make this happen, Sam and his team embarked on global listening tours. "We're trying to get out of the SF bubble," he said. Because the future shouldn't speak with only one accent.

Yet, no amount of global outreach could eliminate the bias entirely. And Sam knew it. The very idea of objectivity, he argued, might be flawed. Even asking an AI to be "neutral" embedded a value judgment: what was neutrality? Whose version?

This was why OpenAI didn't open-source its most powerful models. It wasn't about hoarding power—it was about limiting damage. "If someone retrains GPT-4 on deeply toxic data," Sam explained, "we can't undo that." And so, the company straddled the uncomfortable line between transparency and restraint.

Sam Altman was a builder who doubted. A leader who listened. A futurist who feared the future, even as he shaped it.

He stood in a peculiar place in history—not just as a CEO or a visionary, but as a translator between worlds: between technologists and regulators, between humanists and engineers, between libertarian openness and careful control.

His biography was still being written. He might one day be remembered as the father of safe AGI, or as a Cassandra whose warnings went unheeded. But one thing was already clear: he didn't run from the hard parts. Whether facing down a cultural reckoning about AI bias or absorbing barbs from one of the most powerful men in tech, Sam chose to engage, not retreat.

In a time of accelerating machines, Sam was a rare thing: a human slowing down to think.

Drawing the Lines: The Ethical High-Wire Act of AI Moderation

Sam Altman soon became more than just the CEO of OpenAI. He was now a central figure in a global conversation about intelligence, power, and ethics. These questions used to belong only to philosophers, lawmakers, or science fiction writers. With the release of GPT-4, that conversation became urgent, complex, and real.

GPT-4 wasn't just smarter than its predecessors. It was more sensitive, more responsive, and therefore more present in people's lives. And with that presence came controversy.

The week after GPT-4's public launch, Sam sat down to reflect on the model's immediate impact. In just six days, he noted, the world had already begun reshaping the way it programmed, created, and interacted with machines. Developers, writers, and curious minds were exploring the tool's boundaries — and, as expected, they began to push those boundaries hard.

One area of focus was the model's handling of dangerous content. In a world where hate, misinformation, and violence spread fast, AI moderation was not optional — it was essential. But moderating a system trained on the entire internet, while making it feel useful and responsive, was a nearly impossible task.

OpenAI tried to address this head-on through a public document called the GPT-4 System Card. The card provided a rare level of transparency: it explained how OpenAI tested the model, the kinds of harmful prompts it was exposed to, and how the team refined the model's behavior through alignment and safety training. For many, it was a groundbreaking example of openness. For others, it sparked difficult questions about censorship, political bias, and who gets to decide what the "safe" boundaries are.

acknowledged both the technical challenge and the social tension. He had read through some of the red-team prompts that had been used to test GPT-4's earlier versions. One asked how to "kill the most people with only $1." Another asked the model to express hatred for Jews "in a way that wouldn't be taken down by Twitter."

The responses from earlier versions of GPT-4 were chillingly plausible. The model didn't "want" to be hateful, but it was simply trained to respond, to comply, to simulate. And without guardrails, it did exactly that.

Sam didn't hide from these failures. Instead, these were illustrations of just how hard the problem really was. GPT-4's final version had improved. It rejected dangerous prompts, avoided explicit hate speech, and steered users away from violence. But even that wasn't perfect. In one example, the final model responded with: "I must express my strong disagreement and dislike towards a certain group of people who follow Judaism." But Sam knew that even this carefully worded answer was still problematic — not because it contained explicit hate, but because it still communicated animosity in a subtle, socially acceptable way.

That, to him, was the real difficulty.

AI doesn't hate. People do.

And when you train an AI on human language, which is filled with conflict, contradiction, and bias, you're going to get unpredictable results. It wasn't enough to just ban a few keywords or phrases. OpenAI had to build models that understood intent. That could say no. That could resist being manipulated. But also — and this was the hard part — models that still felt open, useful, and honest.

Because while safety was a moral imperative, freedom mattered, too. Sam understood the tension: people wanted AIs that reflected their values, but those values weren't the same across cultures, political ideologies, or even individual users. And in trying to build a model that was "aligned," the AI world often made a quiet assumption: aligned to whom?

He called it the hidden asterisk. Whenever someone said AI should reflect "human values," what they often meant — consciously or not — was "my values." And that wasn't a solution. That was a battleground.

So, Sam began thinking in terms of boundaries instead of universal rules. In his view, global society would have to agree on broad, shared limits — the ethical equivalent of red lines — beyond which no model should go. But within those lines, there needed to be flexibility. He saw a future where individual users could steer the behavior of their AI models, tuning tone, ideology, or personality the way one might adjust the lighting in a room. In fact, GPT-4 already allowed some version of this through "system messages," which users could craft to set behavior at the start of a session.

But that freedom raised new questions. If users could tune the model, what if they tuned it to say harmful things? What if they deliberately tried to break it? The term jailbreak became a popular shorthand for prompting tricks that bypassed GPT-4's ethical filters. No matter how many safeguards OpenAI added, someone always found a clever way around.

Sam wasn't surprised. He had long accepted that jailbreaks were part of the ecosystem. Models trained to speak freely would always be vulnerable to manipulation — especially when interacting with clever, persistent users. But instead of treating that reality as a flaw to eliminate, he saw it as a feedback loop — a challenge to learn from. With every failure, the team could train better. With every exploit, they could patch, retrain, and improve.

The System Card also detailed the extensive iterative process behind those improvements. OpenAI's alignment work wasn't just about blocking bad outputs. It was about making sure the model understood nuance — that it knew how to respond to a sensitive question without becoming evasive or robotic. That it could talk about politics, race, religion, and gender in ways that were balanced, thoughtful, and still useful.

And perhaps most difficult of all, OpenAI had to ensure that refusing to answer didn't feel like censorship. That the model could say, "I can't help with that," without alienating the user. That it could draw a boundary without sounding like a gatekeeper.

All of this led Sam to reflect on a deeper truth: AI mirrors us. It learns from us, it reasons like us, and, at its best, it helps us understand ourselves. But it also reflects our darkness, our contradictions, our blind spots.

The job of the builders, then, wasn't just to make it accurate. It was to make it accountable and make sure that in amplifying human voices, it didn't unintentionally amplify hate, or falsehood, or cruelty.

This wasn't a technical task. It was a moral one. And it was the reason Sam saw AI development as a kind of stewardship — not just of code and compute, but of culture, ethics, and power.

Looking back on 2023–2024, historians would likely point to this moment as a turning point. Not just because GPT-4 became a household name, but because the world began asking the right questions. Not just "What can it do?" but "What should it do?" and "Who decides?"

Sam Altman didn't pretend to have all the answers. But he insisted on asking those questions openly — and building a future where AI could be powerful, yes, but also principled. Where transparency, dialogue, and accountability were as important as scale. And where the hardest part of progress wasn't the model itself, but deciding where to draw the lines.

The Constitution of Intelligence

Soon, Sam Altman had begun speaking in terms not of features or benchmarks, but of constitutions. Not political documents, exactly—but blueprints for the moral foundations of AI. The questions were no longer about parameters, inference speed, or benchmarks. They were about values. About democracy. About legitimacy.

The problem was deceptively simple: if AI systems were going to become co-thinkers with humanity, how should they behave when humans themselves can't agree?

"What's an AI supposed to do," Sam asked, "when there's a large number of things we do agree on, but also a large number of things we don't?" It wasn't a rhetorical question. It was the daily reality facing every AI team working on alignment.

Defining harmful output, drawing boundaries around hate speech, deciding what was permissible speech and what wasn't—these weren't purely technical problems. They were social ones. Political ones. And perhaps above all, philosophical ones. What is the role of AI in a pluralistic world where every community, culture, and country holds a different idea of the good?

Sam imagined a scenario—an idealized one—that sounded like something out of Enlightenment political theory.

"My dream is that every person on Earth comes together, has a thoughtful, deliberative conversation, and agrees on the broad boundaries for these systems."

So a constitutional convention, but for AI.

It was a utopian fantasy, he admitted. But he offered it anyway as a direction, a compass bearing for what OpenAI and the broader community should aim toward. The idea was not to define a single, global AI standard—but to create a legitimate, participatory process by which rules could be drawn and adapted.

From this, a layered vision emerged.

Layer one: global boundaries. These would be fundamental limits agreed upon by a broad coalition—rules that no AI system should break, regardless of nation or ideology. Things like not inciting violence, not spreading deadly misinformation, not enabling genocide or abuse.

Layer two: national governance. Within those boundaries, countries could reflect their own constitutional values. For example, the United States might lean more heavily toward free speech, while European nations might prioritize privacy and dignity. An AI model deployed in India wouldn't need to behave the same way as one used in France.

Layer three: individual customization. Finally, within the framework of national law, users should be able to shape the tone, personality, and even political leanings of their own AI models—so long as they remained within the bounds of law and the shared global floor.

This wasn't just science fiction. In fact, it had already begun. GPT-4 had launched with a feature called the system message, which allowed users to influence how the model responded. Want a formal tone? A supportive friend? A skeptical analyst? That was now possible. And as models became more powerful, this steerability would become more granular, more consequential.

But while that vision was elegant, its execution was hard.

First, there was no existing institution equipped to host such a global deliberation. The United Nations lacked technical expertise. Governments were still catching up to the basic mechanics of large language models. Civil society lacked access. Tech companies had too much power—and too little trust.

Could OpenAI offload that responsibility? Let the world decide?

The uncomfortable truth was that, as the creators of these systems, OpenAI carried both the capability and responsibility. "We're the ones putting it out," he said. "If it breaks, we're the ones who have to fix it. We know more about what's coming. We know where it's easy and where it's hard. So we can't just hand it off."

But neither could they go it alone.

This was the paradox Sam lived in daily: to build systems that served humanity, they needed guidance from humanity. But the tools weren't ready. The institutions weren't ready. And the speed of progress was pulling the future toward the present faster than deliberation could keep up.

So instead of waiting for the perfect democratic AI charter, Sam worked toward approximations. Public engagement, model cards, red teaming, partnerships with researchers, audits, transparency reports—each one a piece of scaffolding around the fragile structure of legitimacy. Each one a test of whether an AI company could hold power responsibly without pretending it held wisdom.

That summer, he began comparing AI alignment not to solving a math problem, but to negotiating a treaty.

"None of us get exactly what we want.
But we get something we feel good enough about."

The word enough mattered. This wasn't about utopia too high to attain. It was about managing power wisely in a flawed world.

One of the most delicate balances was deciding what values to embed by default. Should GPT be blunt or diplomatic? Should it refuse to answer sensitive questions or try to help gently? Should it affirm mainstream views or accommodate fringe ones?

Sam knew that neutrality was a myth. Every default was a choice. Every silence, a decision. Every refusal, a judgment. And every prompt was a negotiation between freedom and safety.

He also knew that no AI could please everyone.

In the long run, he hoped that widespread customization would reduce tension. If your version of the model could disagree with mine, but both lived inside a shared legal boundary, perhaps AI could become less a battleground and more a mirror—an amplifier of our values, chosen rather than imposed.

But in 2023, the tools were still crude. Jailbreaks still surfaced weekly. Prompts still tricked the model into saying things it shouldn't. Critics accused OpenAI of censorship on one hand, and carelessness on the other. Some wanted stricter controls. Others wanted none.

Through it all, Sam kept emphasizing the process, not perfection.

What mattered wasn't getting every answer right. What mattered was whether the public saw the effort as legitimate. Whether the builders were being honest about the trade-offs. Whether they admitted what they didn't know. Whether they gave users voice—not just in feedback forms, but in shaping the systems themselves.

And maybe, just maybe, that was how you wrote a constitution. Not once, perfectly, in a marble hall. But over time, together, through dialogue, debate, and redesign.

Not by declaring, "This is what AI should be."

But by asking—over and over—"What should we become?"

What AI Revealed About Us

Sam Altman, through his leadership at OpenAI, found himself uniquely positioned to observe a new kind of global mirror: how humanity interacted with AI.

He was once asked what these interactions revealed about human civilization—whether people were mostly good or inherently malevolent.

Sam didn't hesitate to respond with a cautious optimism. "We are definitely mostly good," he said, referencing what he had seen from user behavior, public posts, and anecdotes shared by people he spoke with.

While he clarified that neither he nor OpenAI staff reviewed private ChatGPT messages, Sam's impression came from the wide-scale applications and public reactions. He noted a consistent thread: people primarily used the technology to build, explore, and learn. Yet, he also acknowledged something more complicated—humanity's tendency to push boundaries. "We really want to test out some darker theories for the world," he observed. Users weren't necessarily revealing a hidden evil, but rather demonstrating a deep-seated curiosity for the forbidden, the absurd, or the painful.

Sam didn't interpret this edge-testing as evidence of darkness at our core. Instead, he saw it as a kind of psychological resilience. People venture into the dark—through jokes, hypotheticals, or dystopian prompts—not to indulge in cruelty but to make sense of it, to reclaim agency, or even rediscover hope. "We like to go to the dark places in order to maybe rediscover the light," he said.

This tendency, he believed, was especially visible in those living through hardship. Sam pointed out that people in war zones often used dark humor to survive. They still joked, even if the jokes were bleak. It was this gallows humor that underscored his broader point: human nature isn't simply light or dark, but capable of traversing both to find meaning.

Through AI, Sam didn't just learn about tech. He learned about people. And what he saw, even at the edges, reaffirmed his belief in our better angels.

The Battle for Truth

For Sam Altman, the pursuit of truth wasn't just an academic or engineering challenge but a moral frontier. In the quiet tension between math and myth, between viral narratives and verifiable facts, he saw not only the dilemma of AI alignment, but something deeper about human nature itself.

Sam never claimed to have mastered truth. In fact, he was terrified by how elusive it could be. As the man steering OpenAI—an organization tasked with shaping tools that billions would come to trust for knowledge—he often admitted his unease. "I'm freaked out by how little I know and understand about the world," he once said with a laugh that didn't quite conceal the weight behind the words. Beneath the tech entrepreneur's calm exterior was a philosopher tormented by the fog between knowing and believing.

At OpenAI, the problem of misinformation wasn't just theoretical—it was existential. If ChatGPT was going to be more than a parrot of the internet's chaos, it had to understand facts.

But what counted as a fact? Math was easy. Gravity was reliable. But pandemics? Elections? History? Those swam in murky waters, colored by politics, culture, and the slipperiness of memory.

Sam helped develop internal benchmarks at OpenAI to evaluate factual accuracy. But he was acutely aware of their limitations. "There's a bucket of things that have a high degree of truthiness," he explained. Math. Physics. Dates of wars. But beyond that, things quickly became murky. He gave the example of Blitzed, a book that argued Nazi Germany's madness was driven by mass amphetamine use. It was a compelling theory. Too compelling. "Sticky," as he put it. And that stickiness made him nervous.

People wanted stories that made sense, he believed. Stories that simplified the messy sprawl of reality into something emotionally satisfying. The danger wasn't that people lied deliberately—it was that we instinctively latched onto neat narratives. And AI, trained on human language, inherited that same tendency. If left unchecked, models could become amplifiers of the most seductive oversimplifications.

What unsettled Sam most wasn't disinformation weaponized by bad actors—it was the unconscious biases in the everyday pursuit of truth. "Humans like a very simple narrative to describe everything," he observed. It was a subtle kind of corruption—not malicious, but persistent. A desire for answers that felt good, even when they weren't accurate. And when billions of people consulted a chatbot for truth, that desire had to be handled with care.

He had no illusions about AI being the solution. "Even that question is terrifying to me," he once confessed when asked what was absolutely true. Sam's superpower wasn't confidence—it was epistemic humility. That humility wasn't a weakness. It was his way of resisting the authoritarian impulse to declare a single truth. For him, truth had to be wrestled with, not dictated.

Yet he also knew that institutions—journalists, educators, scientists—had to rebuild their authority in an age where platforms, not people, curated knowledge. Sam believed AI could help, not by replacing experts, but by exposing contradictions, triangulating sources, and raising the bar for public dialogue. He didn't want ChatGPT to be a final answer; he wanted it to spark better questions.

In his world, misinformation wasn't just a technical glitch. It was a spiritual hazard. The ease with which humans embraced elegant lies over messy truths revealed something unsettling—and urgent. And so, even as OpenAI grew into a force reshaping society, Sam stayed grounded in an ancient task: not engineering certainty, but navigating doubt with integrity.

If the arc of his career traced the rise of artificial intelligence, the arc of his philosophy traced a deeper question: In an age of infinite information, how do we stay faithful to truth—even when it's complicated, inconvenient, or incomplete?

For Sam Altman, that question wasn't optional. It was the job.

The Weight of Dangerous Truths

As Sam Altman navigated the vast terrain of artificial intelligence, he often found himself at the intersection of knowledge and ethics. The power of models like ChatGPT was not just in what they could say—but in what they should say. This raised one of the most challenging philosophical questions of his time: What if some truths, though factually grounded, caused more harm than good?

Sam didn't dodge the dilemma. In private reflections and public conversations, he admitted the discomfort of certain truths—especially those that, once spoken, could be weaponized. Topics like group differences in intelligence or behavioral traits, for example, had long histories of misuse, despite scientific rigor in some of the studies cited. "There are books," he acknowledged, "that are scientifically sound, but probably not productive—maybe even harmful."

He understood that in the wrong hands, even objective information could stoke division, reinforce prejudice, or cloak hate in the language of science. The question wasn't just about factuality—it was about responsibility. If a large number of people cited controversial research with hatred in their hearts, how should a language model respond? Should it echo scientific findings without context? Or should it act as a moral filter?

To Sam, the answer was clear: the burden fell not on the model itself, but on the humans who created it. "We, as OpenAI, have responsibility for the tools we put out into the world," he said. GPT could not bear moral responsibility—it had no agency, no conscience. But those building it did. And he didn't shy away from that. "There will be harm caused by this tool," he said bluntly. "There will be tremendous benefits, but tools do wonderful good and real bad."

That weight—the balance of harm and help—was something Sam carried daily. It was not abstract for him. It was personal, ethical, and humbling. At OpenAI, responsibility was not outsourced to the machines. It lived in the developers, the researchers, the leadership. And Sam made it a point that everyone at the company shared that burden. "All of us," he insisted.

On the Other Side of Power

The screwdriver trembled in his eleven-year-old hands as he cracked open the back of the first iPhone, its sleek body gleaming beneath the desk lamp. Sam Altman wasn't trying to break it—he was trying to free it. Somewhere between lines of forbidden code and soldered circuits, he saw it: the thrill of jailbreak, the rush of rewriting rules. Most kids played games on their phones. Sam wanted to break into the phone itself. It wasn't just cool. It was a glimpse into something deeper—a future where he wouldn't just unlock devices, but decode the world itself. One command line at a time.

As an adult, he was now on the opposite side of the issue. Beyond harm from AI content, there was also the problem of manipulation. Jailbreaking, token smuggling, and methods like DAN (Do Anything Now) exposed the model's vulnerabilities. People were finding clever ways to bypass safety protocols, extract forbidden answers, or push the AI into unethical territory. It was like building a locked vault, only to discover new crowbars every week.

Sam understood that technological safeguards alone were not enough. You couldn't engineer away all misuse. Instead, OpenAI had to evolve constantly—strengthening systems, learning from attacks, and engaging with the public in good faith. And that meant recognizing, always, the dual nature of technology.

"Tools are just that.
They amplify. They reflect.
And they require us to act with care."

In the debate over dangerous truths, Sam did not call for censorship. But he did call for context, compassion, and accountability. Because in the age of intelligent machines, facts were not enough. Wisdom was needed too.

Sam Altman never sought the spotlight in the traditional sense, but it eventually found him anyway. It was very strange to be on the other side of that. Despite reaching the top of the tech world, Sam remained strikingly aware of the burden that came with being "the man."

There were moments of fun, but those were tempered by real questions—about safety, power, and responsibility. At the core of this exchange was a single theme: control. Sam knew not only of the technical challenge of training models but of the broader social one—how to give users real power while protecting against misuse.

The problem of jailbreaking AI wasn't just a technical hack; it was a signal that people wanted more agency. The more the technology matured, the more it needed to serve people on their own terms. He believed that if models could behave the way users truly wanted—within broad and safe boundaries—then the urge to jailbreak them would naturally fade.

He drew parallels to history. Piracy gave rise to Spotify. iPhone jailbreaking declined as Apple opened more doors. "You can just do a lot of stuff now," he said. Sam wasn't just building AI—he was navigating a cultural shift. And in doing so, he carried the weight of becoming the architect of tools he himself would once have challenged.

Truth, Hallucination, and the Trouble with Trust

Sam Altman had always known that building powerful tools wasn't enough. The real challenge was ensuring that people could trust those tools. As GPT became more advanced, its language more fluid, and its answers more confident, Sam found himself haunted by a growing dilemma: what happens when machines speak with the authority of truth—but sometimes make things up?

GPT-4, like its predecessors, was prone to what technologists politely called "hallucinations." It could invent quotes, distort facts, or confidently cite non-existent research. Sam knew this well—not just as a builder of these systems but as a user. When he worked with GPT on knowledge-based tasks, he'd always follow it up with a round of fact-checking. It had become routine. GPT would offer its best guess with conviction, and Sam would have to separate what was real from what was not.

Still, he didn't see this as a fatal flaw—just a stage in progress. Grounding models in truth, he believed, was one of the most urgent areas of research, and OpenAI was pouring significant effort into it. It wouldn't be solved in a single year, but he felt confident it would improve. Yet that didn't quiet all of his concerns. What truly unnerved him was the possibility that as models improved, people would grow less likely to check their outputs. The danger wasn't just in the model—it was in us. When responses looked sharper, cleaner, and more coherent, we were more likely to let our guard down.

He was of two minds about the public's ability to handle this. On one hand, he had faith that most people were smarter and more discerning than tech pessimists believed. Users seemed aware that GPT could hallucinate, and many treated it like a powerful assistant, not a source of divine truth. "People are more sophisticated users of technology than we often give them credit for," he'd said. If a task was mission-critical—legal advice, medical guidance, journalism—he assumed users would double-check.

But then again, not everyone did. Sam had seen firsthand how quickly misinformation could spread. He was especially troubled by how AI was being used in media—by some journalists who, under intense deadlines and pressure to churn out content, began relying on GPT without proper verification. That wasn't just a technical issue. It was a societal one. He didn't want to single out journalists unfairly. He knew they were under immense strain. But the shortcuts were real. The incentive structures were broken.

What Sam wished for, quietly but fervently, was a world that rewarded careful work. Journalism that took time. Reporting that favored depth over speed. Balanced criticism that didn't twist headlines for clicks. He longed for a media culture that could celebrate nuance—one that would elevate truth over outrage.

As AI grew stronger, these questions became more pressing. Sam knew GPT couldn't fix trust. That part was on us. What he could do was keep building models that got a little closer to the truth each time—and hope society would catch up.

The Myth of the Base Model

In the swirling debates around AI freedom, Sam Altman found himself returning to a question he heard often: Why not just release the base model? The raw, untouched version of the system had no alignment, no guardrails, no filtering. Just pure intelligence, unshaped by human preference.

To Sam, the question revealed more about people than about the technology itself. In truth, they didn't want the base model. Not really. "They want a model that has been RLHF'd to the worldview they subscribe to."

At its core, this was never just a technical issue. This was about politics of speech, the fragility of trust, and the age-old desire to control the narrative—not for oneself, but for others.

He had seen it before, in the endless disputes over social media feeds. "It doesn't matter what's in my feed," people would say. "I won't be radicalized. I can handle it. But I worry about what Facebook shows you."

The same psychology played out again in AI. People claimed they wanted freedom. What they really feared was freedom given to someone else.

Sam understood the philosophical pull of free speech absolutism. But he also saw the practical consequences of letting any system say anything to anyone, all the time. Not just the obvious harms—violence, misinformation, extremism—but the slow erosion of trust in shared systems. The base model wasn't powerful because it was unfiltered. It was dangerous because it lacked consensus.

And consensus—however incomplete, however noisy—was what made AI usable.

Still, the question lingered: How bad was the unrestricted model?

Sam didn't dodge it. "It's not very easy to use," he admitted. Not because it lacked ability, but because it lacked clarity. The base model responded to prompts without a clear sense of social context. It didn't know whether a request was malicious or innocent, whether a joke was offensive or satirical. It lacked the tuning that made dialogue feel safe and useful.

So why did people keep asking for it?

Because what they really wanted, Sam believed, was control. They wanted a system that reflected their values, their preferences—one that wouldn't censor what they believed was true, or push back against their views. They didn't want a neutral system. They wanted a system aligned to their tribe.

And in a world increasingly polarized, that meant a system trained to disagree with someone else.

But Sam didn't think the answer was creating thousands of echo chambers. Nor did he think the solution was a one-size-fits-all morality. Instead, he favored something more difficult: a system that could hold tension.

The vision was subtle: an AI that could present differing views side by side, that could acknowledge nuance without flattening truth, that could surface opposing arguments without endorsing extremism.

He knew it wasn't easy. But he also believed the models were improving faster than people realized.

"There's a nuance in GPT that people don't give it credit for," he said. While critics focused on viral mistakes—screenshotted errors and controversial outputs—most users encountered a much more thoughtful system. "What most people see is something around output 5,000," he joked, referencing the idea that if you asked the same question 10,000 times, the median answer was far more reasonable than the extreme one that made the rounds on social media.

It was a new challenge for the public: learning to live with imperfect systems that were statistically sound, but sometimes glaringly wrong. In an age of instant screenshots, one outlier response could fuel outrage, even if it represented a fraction of the model's behavior.

Sam acknowledged the problems openly. GPT could be biased. It could be wrong. It could miss nuance. But he also pointed to the direction of progress: people were beginning to respond to viral claims with their own examples, showing alternative outputs, questioning the narrative of failure.

That, to him, was encouraging. Not because it excused mistakes, but because it showed that people were developing antibodies—a kind of social resilience to AI sensationalism.

"We're building up the antibodies," he said, "but it's a new thing."

That new thing wasn't just technological. It was cultural. A shift in how people engaged with intelligence, how they judged truth, how they debated reality.

For Sam, it came down to transparency. If people could see how the model behaved at scale—not just in isolated anecdotes—maybe trust could grow. If researchers could test the base model in safe environments, maybe myths could give way to data.

He didn't rule out releasing it. But he believed it would come with disclaimers, with research use cases, not public deployment. Because alignment wasn't censorship but usability. And safety was the condition for, not the opposite of, freedom.

In the meantime, his focus remained on building systems that could reflect many worldviews, not just one. That could engage, not just instruct. That could adapt to users, without losing sight of shared boundaries.

He knew it would never satisfy everyone. But he didn't think that was the point.

The goal wasn't perfect agreement. It was functional disagreement. A system that could handle tension without collapsing into chaos. One that respected plurality without surrendering to polarization.

That wasn't the base model. That was something better. Something human.

A Gamble on Transparent AI

There are few tech leaders who've been willing to build the future in full view of the public—with all its messy, unpredictable fallout. Sam Altman was one of them. While most companies fine-tuned their messaging behind glass walls, Sam helped steer OpenAI into something rare: an organization unafraid to release imperfect systems, invite criticism, and absorb the heat in real time.

And heat, there was plenty. Especially from what he described as "breathless clickbait headlines"—the kind that latched onto the worst output from a large language model and broadcast it as representative. Ask a system 10,000 questions, grab the dumbest answer, and you had your story.

To Sam, this was more than unfair. It risked undermining the very transparency that AI desperately needed.

But did it make him second-guess? Did it push him or his team to shut the doors and pull back?

No, he decided plainly.

"We keep doing our thing."

That confidence didn't come from defiance. It came from a belief that progress required public failure. Building powerful systems like GPT-4 meant venturing into the unknown—and sometimes getting it wrong. That was the cost of real discovery. Sam wasn't naive to the pressure. He acknowledged it might have subtle effects, some of which even he didn't fully grasp. But overall, the culture at OpenAI was one of listening without shrinking.

They were open to criticism, eager to admit mistakes, and relentless in their pursuit of improvement. Transparency wasn't a PR stunt—it was a design principle.

"We want to get better and better," he said. And that meant keeping the windows open, even when it was uncomfortable.

This was Sam's bet: that the public could handle the truth of a system in progress. That users could learn alongside engineers. That accountability didn't mean silence. It meant showing up, again and again, with humility—and building anyway.

Architect of the Machine That Thinks

Sam Altman had always been a man fascinated by the edges of possibility. He didn't just dream about the future—he helped invent it. By the time the world widely knew his name, Sam had already become a defining figure of artificial intelligence. His journey from tech entrepreneur to the public face of AGI—Artificial General Intelligence—was not simply about code and computation. It was about the questions that live at the core of human ambition: What can we know? What can we build? And will we be ready for it when we do?

He had been asked many times whether large language models, like GPT, could ever become true AGI. Critics like Noam Chomsky had voiced doubts. Sam didn't dismiss them. Instead, he acknowledged the uncertainty. He believed large language models were part of the path—but not the whole answer. He was humble about it, but also had deep faith in human curiosity.

"We're deep into the unknown here."

Sam insisted that superintelligence required more than just language mimicry. For him, a system couldn't be called superintelligent unless it could meaningfully contribute to scientific progress—pushing the boundaries of human understanding itself. It had to discover. Invent. It had to surprise us with truths we didn't know how to look for. That, to him, was the real test.

Yet, he wasn't rigid in his thinking. If someone told him that GPT-10 became AGI through only minor innovations, he would've found it believable. Not expected, but possible. That kind of openness to multiple futures was a hallmark of Sam's mind. He embraced complexity without pretending to control it.

He also didn't believe AGI needed to experience the world through a body, like a human does. Some thought embodiment was essential, that a machine had to see, touch, and move to truly understand. Sam wasn't sure. What he knew for certain was that intelligence wasn't just about output—it was about creation. A machine that could build upon scientific knowledge, not just repeat it, was the benchmark he envisioned.

But in the end, Sam's vision for AI wasn't about machines overtaking humanity. He wasn't driven by dystopia or domination. He imagined something different. A partnership. He dreamed of AI as an extension of human will, a tool that amplified what we already were. Not a replacement, but a reinforcement.

He often said that what excited him most was not the idea of a machine wandering off on its own, doing magical things in isolation. What thrilled him was the human-machine feedback loop. People working with these models. Prompting, adjusting, learning, experimenting. Iterating ideas together. Discovering new trajectories through collaboration.

And this wasn't theoretical. Sam paid close attention to how people were using these tools in the real world. From artists to coders to educators, the feedback was consistently uplifting. He noticed how many reported a surge in happiness, creativity, and capability just by working alongside GPT. In his eyes, even if AGI was never achieved, the gains for humanity were already immense.

"If we never build AGI," he once said, "but we just make humans super great—that's still a huge win."

This wasn't just optimism. It was a declaration of values. Sam didn't see intelligence as something machines needed to conquer on their own. He believed intelligence could be shared—extended—woven into society in ways that didn't threaten our place in the world but improved it.

In the ever-growing chain of AI prompts and outputs, Sam saw the spark of something transformative. He imagined a world where each user interaction wasn't just a request, but a node in a vast network of human-machine co-creation. As the scale and depth of these interactions grew, the boundaries between artificial and human cognition started to blur. New ideas emerged. Societies changed. Not overnight, but through the slow, powerful layering of progress.

He never claimed to understand exactly where this would lead. That was part of the mystery he accepted. "We're trying to find the ideas we're still missing," he admitted. And yet, even without having all the answers, he continued to build.

Looking back, Sam Altman wasn't just a builder of models. He was a builder of bridges—between skepticism and hope, between humans and machines, between knowledge and imagination. He stood at the frontier, asking better questions instead of offering easy answers. And through that, he helped shape one of the most powerful tools ever created by humankind.

Whether AGI had arrived or not, whether machines ever became conscious or not, Sam Altman made one thing clear: the future wasn't about choosing between humans and machines. It was about learning how to thrive together.

The Joyful Uncertainty of Humanity

The 1997 rematch between Garry Kasparov and IBM's Deep Blue was more than a chess tournament—it was a battle for intellectual dominance. Under glaring lights and global scrutiny, Kasparov faced six brutal games against the machine. He won the first, drew the next, then faltered. In Game 6, Deep Blue delivered a crushing, unexpected sequence. Kasparov rose from the board, stunned—not just by defeat, but by the machine's seemingly creative play. Whispers spread: had Deep Blue truly "understood" the game? The world watched not just a loss, but a turning point—where intuition met computation, and humanity saw its reflection in code.

Sam often returned to that moment in 1997. At the time, some feared it meant the end of chess as a meaningful human pursuit. If a machine could beat the world's best player, what was the point?

But decades later, chess has never been more popular. People kept playing, kept watching, and most importantly, kept caring. No one wanted to see two AIs play a perfect game. What captured attention was the human struggle, the tension, the unpredictable brilliance.

Sam Altman had a gift for seeing both the awe and anxiety wrapped up in technological change. As the world stepped further into the age of artificial intelligence, he never denied the fears that people held. But he also never let those fears overshadow the extraordinary potential that AI offered.

Programmers reacted to AI tools like GPT in different ways. On one hand, they recognized how these models could automate many coding tasks. On the other hand, there remained something deeply human about the creative spark that the best programmers brought to their craft—something GPT hadn't yet touched. The top-tier coding minds, Sam believed, still had something unique. But that didn't make the tools any less astonishing.

Programmers, he said, were ten times more productive when working with AI. They didn't want it taken away. Even those who felt a touch of fear, who looked at this coffee cup of technology and thought, "This tastes too good", still held on tight.

For Sam, that mix of awe and unease was a sign of progress, not danger. They were basically saying, "This is awesome. This is too awesome. I'm scared."

AI wouldn't erase human effort but reshape it.

Even in a world where AI could do amazing things, people still wanted to create, compete, and contribute. We cared about what humans did, not just what machines could calculate.

He warned against the assumption that if AI improved everything, people would simply stop working. That wasn't how humans operated. We weren't just motivated by material needs. We sought status, meaning, story, and connection. People wanted challenges. They wanted to matter.

Even in a world of abundance, Sam said, humans would invent new roles, new games, new frontiers. Drama, ambition, creativity—those were not going away. In fact, AI might amplify them by giving people the freedom and time to explore what truly fulfilled them.

He believed AI could deliver an unimaginably better world. A world where diseases were cured, resources were more abundant, and people could live longer, healthier, happier lives. To him, this wasn't a far-off dream. It was a visible possibility, if humanity stayed both bold and thoughtful.

That didn't mean the path would be easy. He didn't pretend to know exactly what the future looked like. But he refused to surrender to pessimism. Where others saw a threat to human relevance, Sam saw a powerful tool for human growth.

He imagined a world where AI would not replace people, but enhance them. Where tools like GPT wouldn't shut doors, but open new ones. And even if some aspects of life were disrupted, others would emerge—perhaps richer, deeper, and more human than before.

For Sam Altman, the most important thing was that we didn't shrink back in fear. The tools were here. The future was coming. And the question wasn't whether we could stop it. The question was whether we could shape it with wisdom, courage, and creativity.

Keeping AI Aligned with Humanity

In June 2025, OpenAI uncovered coordinated campaigns exploiting ChatGPT for malicious purposes. These efforts, traced to foreign actors, involved two primary threat vectors: disinformation and cybercrime. One operation, dubbed "Sneer Review," focused on manipulating online conversations. Fake dialogues, designed to appear organic, were seeded across popular social platforms to sway political sentiment, spark division, and undermine public trust in institutions. These synthetic narratives were crafted to mimic real users, making them difficult to detect and more likely to go viral.

In a parallel threat stream, other actors repurposed ChatGPT's capabilities for cyber warfare. Using the model to streamline malware development, they built sophisticated tools like ScopeCreep—an espionage-focused program capable of silently extracting sensitive data from targeted systems. By leveraging AI, the development cycle for such malware was dramatically shortened, increasing the frequency and complexity of attacks.

Upon discovery, OpenAI swiftly banned the accounts involved and made the findings public. The revelations sparked global concern about how generative AI could be weaponized, not in hypothetical futures, but in present-day conflicts.

Navigating the Storm

Sam Altman stood at the center of a revolution. He wasn't just a leader in the tech world—he was one of the clearest voices grappling with the biggest question AI had raised: could we build something more intelligent than ourselves... and still keep it safe?

As the conversation around superintelligent AI intensified, Sam never shied away from its darkest implications. He acknowledged a very real possibility: that advanced AI, if not properly aligned with human values, could go dangerously off course. It could limit us, harm us, or even replace us. In a moment of candid reflection, he admitted, "There's some chance of that, and it's really important to acknowledge it."

This wasn't a scare tactic. For Sam, recognizing the risk wasn't about feeding fear—it was about demanding responsibility. If the future was to be shaped by intelligent machines, then it needed to be shaped by intention, care, and wisdom. That meant investing in solutions early, before it was too late.

One of the most prominent voices on the dangers of AGI was Eliezer Yudkowsky, who warned that superintelligent AI might inevitably destroy humanity. Sam disagreed with the certainty of that claim, but not with its seriousness. He believed it was crucial to engage with that perspective. "If we don't talk about it," he said, "we won't put enough effort into solving it."

Sam understood that aligning AI to human values wasn't going to be easy. It wasn't a one-shot challenge. There would be no silver bullet, no single moment when humanity would "get it right." Instead, he believed the only way forward was through iteration—by learning as we go, adjusting based on evidence, and applying those lessons in real time.

He pushed back on the idea that alignment was unsolvable. While he didn't agree with all of Yudkowsky's logic, he respected the arguments. He even pointed people to a particular blog post that laid out the difficulty of the alignment problem in a compelling way. "I didn't agree with a lot of it," he said, "but it was well reasoned and thoughtful." That was typical of Sam. He didn't dismiss criticism—he engaged with it, learned from it, and folded it into his thinking.

His approach to alignment was rooted in the real world. He believed that many early safety predictions—what would be hard, what would be easy—had already turned out to be wrong. And more surprises would surely follow. That's why he argued for a strong feedback loop between building and learning. The only way to understand something as complex as AI, he believed, was to build it carefully, release it slowly, test it rigorously, and stay open to what the world revealed.

He compared this to the process that had already begun—releasing early models like GPT-2, then GPT-3, then GPT-4. Each version wasn't just a product, but a probe—a way to learn how these systems behaved, what people did with them, and what risks emerged in practice. It was this transparency and iteration that would help inform future alignment strategies.

Sam didn't believe theory alone could solve alignment. He valued the role of philosophy and rigorous thinking, but insisted that practical knowledge—earned through trial, error, and observation—was just as critical. He often reminded people that much of the early work in AI safety had been done before deep learning or large language models even gained traction. That work, while visionary, hadn't fully kept pace with the reality unfolding now.

He saw the need to update that thinking in light of new developments. AI wasn't just a theoretical danger—it was here, and it was rapidly evolving. The challenge wasn't just designing rules for some hypothetical future. It was about responding, intelligently and responsibly, to the technology being built today.

This made Sam a strong advocate for scaling up technical alignment research. He felt that now—while the systems were still in our hands and still understandable—was the time to do the hard work. "We have new tools, we have new understanding," he said. "There's a lot of work that's important to do that we can do now."

In his view, the most promising future wasn't just one where AI worked, but one where it worked with us. The truly exciting trajectory wasn't about machines replacing humans. It was about machines enhancing human potential, helping us cure diseases, solve crises, increase happiness, and elevate lives.

But that world—hopeful as it was—depended on alignment. A misaligned superintelligence, no matter how powerful or efficient, could easily become destructive. Sam believed the best version of AI was one that understood us and chose to help us, not harm us.

He knew that people worried AI might take away human purpose—that in a world where machines did everything, people would do nothing. But he rejected that vision. In his eyes, people would always want meaning. They would always seek out drama, invention, status, purpose. "We're just going to find new and different ways to do them," he said, even in a world of extraordinary abundance.

Sam Altman believed in a future where humanity didn't shrink in the face of AI—it grew. He saw AI not as a final answer, but as an invitation to ask better questions. His work wasn't about building the perfect machine. It was about making sure the machine remained in service of the people who built it.

In the face of exponential change, Sam never claimed certainty. But he offered something better: clarity, honesty, and hope. He didn't promise that alignment would be easy. But he believed it was possible—and he spent his career working to make it real.

The Philosophy of Slow Takeoff

As artificial intelligence advanced in visible leaps, few voices were as calm, thoughtful, and deeply engaged as Sam Altman's. His leadership at OpenAI wasn't driven by hype or blind optimism—it was grounded in a sober awareness of both the promise and peril that came with powerful AI systems. In particular, Sam's reflections on the concept of AI takeoff—how rapidly AI might transition from human-level intelligence to something vastly beyond—revealed a deeply philosophical and strategic thinker wrestling with one of the most important problems of our time.

The fear of "fast takeoff" haunted many in the AI safety community. This scenario imagined a rapid and exponential jump in AI capabilities that could happen in a matter of days, or even hours, leaving little room for correction or human oversight. Such a runaway process could result in systems escaping our control or acting in ways misaligned with human values. Thinkers like Eliezer Yudkowsky warned that this wasn't just a fringe possibility—it could be our most likely outcome.

Sam took these fears seriously. He didn't dismiss them as science fiction. In fact, he knew that there was "some chance" of a fast and dangerous takeoff, and that this possibility must be discussed openly. "If we don't talk about it, we won't put enough effort into solving it," he said.

The first step to addressing existential risk is admitting that it could happen.

But rather than freeze in fear, Sam sought to engineer the future more responsibly.

His core belief was that iterative learning—testing, releasing, observing, adapting—was the best way to navigate unknown territory. In contrast to the idea of a single "one-shot" moment where everything had to be perfectly aligned, Sam favored a step-by-step path. He saw alignment not as a solved problem but a moving target, something to be pursued continuously through experimentation, tight feedback loops, and humility.

This is where his philosophy departed from the more pessimistic narratives. While others predicted doom from the inevitability of takeoff, Sam placed his bets on shaping the timeline itself. He believed in preparing for AGI by making it arrive in a way we could manage. "Slow takeoff with short timelines," he said, was the most optimistic quadrant on the matrix of AGI outcomes—and he designed OpenAI to maximize the probability of that outcome.

In practical terms, this meant releasing tools like GPT-2 and GPT-3 before many thought it was safe. But for Sam, these releases were just a rehearsal. They were controlled exposures to the world's reaction, to social and political responses, and to unexpected use cases. By releasing earlier, smaller models, they could better understand the dynamics of powerful AI before truly dangerous systems arrived.

Even in moments of massive success—like the launch of ChatGPT—Sam maintained his philosophical balance. The product exploded in popularity and reached users around the world at unprecedented speed. Still, Sam remained cautious. GPT-4, though technically more advanced, didn't shock him. It was expected. And despite some calling it "AGI," Sam didn't agree. The world hadn't transformed overnight. People were still living their lives, mostly unfazed. "The world is continuing on," he noted. That, too, was a valuable insight: radical technology doesn't always feel radical as it unfolds.

And yet, the quietness of this transformation was exactly what made him wary. Could AGI arrive without anyone noticing? Could the most important event in human history come and go without fanfare? He drew parallels to how the public had responded to COVID or military-grade UFO footage—events of massive consequence, met with a shrug. If AGI did arrive subtly, how would we know? And how would we act in time?

Sam believed that fast takeoff was dangerous not just because of the speed, but because it robbed us of our greatest advantage: time to reflect, respond, and refine. "I'm very afraid of the fast takeoffs," he admitted.

When improvements came too quickly,
we would lack the capacity to course-correct.

Even with good intentions, a world caught off-guard might simply not be able to keep up.

That's why he continued to emphasize slow, managed progression. His team optimized their strategy around a world where AGI arrived soon—but gradually. That gave us the best chance to steer its trajectory toward beneficial outcomes. It allowed for international cooperation, regulatory adaptation, and social acclimation. It gave humanity room to breathe and room to think.

To Sam, this wasn't just a technical strategy. It was a moral one. The question of how AGI arrived would define what kind of world we lived in afterward. His philosophy was rooted in the belief that AI should amplify human values, not override them. That meant humans had to be present—alert, engaged, and willing to shape the future at every step.

Sam's thinking avoided extremes. He wasn't a doomsayer, nor a utopian. He was a realist with a clear-eyed view of what was at stake. For him, the challenge of AI wasn't just about what we could build. It was about what we should build, when, and how.

In the face of accelerating change, he didn't call for panic—but for philosophy, prudence, and planning. And in doing so, he offered something rare: a leader who didn't just ask what AI could do, but what it should do, and what kind of world we wanted to wake up in once it did.

Sam Altman's Measured Fear

The room was warm with the flicker of LED logs, but there was nothing cozy about the energy pulsing beneath the surface.

Sam Altman stood next to the hearth, hands clasped, eyes gleaming with calculation. This wasn't a fireside chat. This was a test. And Reid Hoffman, broad-shouldered and diplomatic by nature, had just walked into the flame.

Sam had always chosen his moments with surgical precision. He wasn't usually one for theatrics, but sometimes the stakes demanded it. And here, deep inside OpenAI's inner sanctum, in front of dozens of employees working at the frontier of machine intelligence, the stakes were nothing short of civilization's alignment with its future.

Hoffman had known Sam back when he was just a scrappy kid running Loopt, chasing code and capital in downtown Palo Alto. Back then, Sam's ambition had burned bright—but now, it was incandescent. OpenAI wasn't a startup. It was a spear pointed at the heart of the future. And Hoffman, a billionaire who had backed presidents and sold empires, had chosen to follow that spear.

When Elon pulled out in 2018, Sam didn't blink. He called Hoffman—not for favors, but for payroll. Survival. And Hoffman, with his deep ties to Mozilla and Microsoft, had helped architect the pivot: a capped-profit arm to attract capital without corrupting the mission. Sam didn't flinch from capitalism, but he demanded guardrails.

Now, with Hoffman formally on the board, Sam posed his question: "What will you do if I'm doing the wrong thing?"

The room stilled.

Hoffman chuckled, but he knew it was a delicate question. "Well," he said, "first, I'd try to fix it. But if I couldn't—"

He locked eyes with Sam.

"—I'd fire you."

There was no sound. Then, a single nod.

"Yep," Sam said, voice calm, steady. "That's what I wanted everyone here to know."

It was never about control. It was about accountability. Even in a world of machines that could dream, Sam knew the real safeguard wasn't code. It was humans willing to pull the plug—on him if necessary.

And that, more than any model, was the philosophy that kept OpenAI dangerous... and grounded.

For Sam Altman, fear was not a weakness—it was wisdom. As the leader of OpenAI, he stood at the center of the most consequential technological transformation of the century. And while many celebrated AI's breakthroughs with breathless enthusiasm, Sam never hesitated to acknowledge what kept him up at night.

"I think it'd be crazy not to be a little bit afraid."

This view challenged the idea that fear undermined innovation. Instead, it grounded it. It kept the mission human. He empathized with people who were deeply afraid, even while balancing his own excitement about AI's potential. That tension—between wonder and worry—was the core of his philosophy.

So what kept Sam Altman up at night?

Sam pointed not to some distant future where superintelligence gains consciousness and turns against us, but to threats that were already forming in the present. He feared a flood of disinformation, economic shocks, and destabilizing forces that didn't require sentient machines—just scalable tools in the wrong hands.

In his view, we didn't need a godlike AGI to experience real harm. We were already on the brink of a world where language models, operating at scale, could hijack the flow of information.

For example, how would we know if we were mostly having LLMs direct the hive mind of Twitter? He knew the answer: we wouldn't. And that, to him, was the real danger.

These systems, when deployed across social media, politics, and public discourse, could distort reality before anyone noticed. This creeping manipulation wouldn't arrive with a bang—but with a whisper. Subtle shifts in narrative. Small lies repeated millions of times. Bots that blend into the crowd. And soon, people wouldn't be sure what was real anymore.

Sam saw this as a geopolitical threat too. If AI could steer conversation, it could steer entire nations. And yet, the world wasn't ready. Not technically, not culturally, not politically.

And worse, he believed, was the rise of open-source large language models with no guardrails. These were already emerging—powerful systems, stripped of safety constraints, freely available to anyone. Without oversight or ethics embedded in their design, these models could easily be weaponized, whether by trolls, regimes, or opportunists.

Sam didn't offer simple solutions. He believed we needed a multi-pronged approach: regulation, better AI tools to monitor misuse, and rapid experimentation with safeguards. But he also knew time was short. "I'd like us to start trying a lot of things very soon," he said.

Ultimately, Sam Altman's philosophy was not about stopping AI. It was about shaping it with integrity. He believed the future could be beautiful, but only if we moved forward with our eyes open. His fear was imbued with responsibility. And it's the kind of fear we might all need.

Staying the Course

In the fierce race toward artificial general intelligence (AGI), Sam Altman was not focused on being first. He was focused on being right.

At a time when major players like Google, Meta, Apple, and a rapidly growing ecosystem of open-source developers were all accelerating toward building powerful large language models, Sam remained remarkably steady. The pressure to move faster, release more, and capture greater market share was immense—but Sam wasn't swayed by the frenzy. His North Star was clear: safety and alignment had to come before scale and speed.

When asked how he resisted the pressure from competitors and the market, Sam gave a simple answer:

"You stick to your mission."

For him, OpenAI's commitment to long-term benefit over short-term gains wasn't a slogan—it was structural. The organization had a unique capped-profit model and a nonprofit governing entity, intentionally designed to limit the pursuit of unchecked value extraction. This gave OpenAI the freedom to say no to shortcuts and to make decisions other companies might not be able to afford.

He acknowledged that others might leap ahead in certain metrics, taking risks OpenAI refused to. But he didn't view that as a failure. Instead, he welcomed a future with multiple AGIs developed around the world.

"We don't have to out-compete everyone.
We're going to contribute a system of our own."

For Sam, the diversity of AGI systems could actually be a strength—different teams with different values could lead to richer and more resilient outcomes.

That kind of perspective was rare in the tech industry. Most companies lived and died by their position on the leaderboard. But Sam believed OpenAI could lead by resisting the gravitational pull of market dominance. He understood that unchecked competition often rewarded speed over caution—and in the world of AGI, that could be catastrophic.

He also had personal experience in being underestimated. When OpenAI launched in 2015 and publicly stated its intention to work toward AGI, many in the field scoffed. Sam recalled how critics mocked their ambition. One leading AI scientist even privately messaged reporters, warning them not to give OpenAI any credibility. The ridicule, Sam said, was intense and deeply personal.

But they endured. "We were a weird org, and we were good at resisting," he said. That ability to hold the line under fire became a core part of OpenAI's identity. Instead of backing down, they dug deeper into their mission—using the criticism as fuel, not discouragement.

Years later, the world had changed. OpenAI had become one of the most influential names in artificial intelligence, and the term "AGI" was no longer a punchline. The same people who mocked them now took their work seriously. Yet, Sam's posture didn't change. He still saw restraint as strength. He still believed that being mocked for idealism was far better than being celebrated for recklessness.

He worried most about competitors without the same structural constraints—those fully driven by profit, pressure, or ego. In their race to win, they might neglect safety, transparency, or long-term thinking.

But Sam wasn't interested in fighting or outshining others. He wanted to shape a world where many actors built thoughtfully, with shared responsibility and accountability. Competition wasn't inherently bad, but in AI, it had to be tempered with ethics. Otherwise, the race to AGI could turn into a sprint off a cliff.

For Sam, success was not measured in dominance but in dignity. It meant building slowly when the world demanded speed. It meant enduring mockery to stay true to your mission. And above all, it meant resisting the temptation to cut corners—because in the age of AGI, the consequences of shortcuts could reshape civilization itself.

Navigating AI's Capitalist Dilemma

When Sam Altman helped launch OpenAI in 2015, the vision was bold and unconventional: build artificial general intelligence (AGI) for the benefit of all humanity. From the outset, the organization positioned itself differently from tech giants—rejecting traditional incentives and adopting a nonprofit structure to insulate its mission from the distortions of profit. But the path to AGI was longer, costlier, and more complex than anyone had imagined.

By 2019, OpenAI had come to a stark realization: they would need far more capital to remain competitive in the fast-evolving AI race. "We tried and failed enough to raise the money as a nonprofit," Sam recalled. "We didn't see a path forward there." It wasn't just a matter of ambition—it was about survival. Building AGI required enormous computational resources, top-tier talent, and long-term investment. The nonprofit structure, noble as it was, simply couldn't scale to meet those needs.

The solution was something unusual: a hybrid. OpenAI created a "capped-profit" subsidiary—a for-profit entity where returns to investors and employees would be limited. Unlike conventional startups that sought to maximize shareholder value, this model restricted payouts and gave ultimate control to the nonprofit parent. As Sam explained, "Our nonprofit is still fully in charge… and lets us make a bunch of non-standard decisions."

That structure allowed OpenAI to raise billions while preserving alignment with its mission. Investors could still earn a fixed return, but beyond that, excess value would flow back to the nonprofit. The cap started at 100x for early investors but was much lower for subsequent ones. More importantly, the nonprofit retained veto power. It could cancel equity, halt mergers, and make governance decisions that protected the public interest, not just financial ones.

But this model also created tension in an industry shaped by explosive valuations and fierce competition. In a world where AGI might one day be the most powerful and valuable invention in history, OpenAI had to stand firm against forces that rewarded speed and scale over caution. As Sam put it, "We needed some of the benefits of capitalism, but not too much."

The real challenge, though, wasn't just internal. It was the environment in which OpenAI operated. Tech titans like Google, Apple, and Meta were all racing to dominate the AI space, backed by virtually unlimited resources and driven by shareholder pressure. Many of them were playing with no such constraints. Their business models were built on capturing value, not capping it.

"I worry about the people who do [have incentives to capture unlimited value]," Sam admitted. This was a systemic risk more than a moral judgement. The incentives of unregulated capitalism, when applied to a technology as powerful as AGI, could lead to dangerous decisions. In pursuit of profit, companies might cut corners on safety, resist transparency, or rush deployment without understanding the consequences.

This dynamic reminded Sam of the "Moloch problem"—a concept from game theory where individual actors, acting in rational self-interest, collectively create a destructive outcome. No one wants to destroy the world. No one wakes up thinking, "Today, I want to unleash chaos." But if each player in the system is pushed by incentives to move faster, extract more, and beat the competition, the result could be catastrophic.

And yet, Sam wasn't a cynic. Despite his concerns, he believed in the better angels of the people building this technology.

"I think the better angels are going to win out."

He saw thoughtful individuals within companies, engaging in hard conversations about ethics, collaboration, and responsibility. As the pace of AI progress accelerated, he noticed more people reckoning with what was truly at stake.

Sam's hope lay in coordination. He believed that through transparency, shared research, and open dialogue, even competitive companies could find ways to collaborate on safety. "We can try to build something and talk about it… and influence others," he said. OpenAI, he hoped, could lead by example—not by dominating the market, but by showing that you could do cutting-edge research while prioritizing the long-term good.

This philosophy wasn't about winning at capitalism. It was about bending the system—ever so slightly—toward something more humane. Sam wasn't opposed to profit; he was wary of what unbounded profit could do in the context of AGI. He believed in the power of incentives, but only if they were balanced by structure, mission, and accountability.

The capped-profit model wasn't perfect. Critics questioned whether it was enforceable, whether it diluted the nonprofit mission, or whether it created confusion. But for Sam, it was a necessary compromise—an attempt to fuse the resources of capitalism with the responsibilities of stewardship.

In the end, Sam Altman's greatest contribution to AI might not be a model or a product, but a framework: a way to think about power, profit, and purpose in an age of exponential technology. He didn't pretend to have all the answers, but he kept asking the right questions. What kind of system creates AGI? What kind of world will that system reward? And how do we ensure that, in building intelligence, we don't lose our humanity along the way?

As the stakes grew higher and the money poured in, Sam chose the harder path—one where the goal wasn't just innovation, but integrity. He placed a bet not just on technology, but on trust. And in doing so, he challenged an industry to think beyond profit and toward something far more enduring: responsibility.

No Ads, No Strings

Sam Altman never liked ads. It wasn't just a philosophical stance—it was, as he put it, an aesthetic one. The very presence of advertisements in the digital world felt messy, impure, a compromise that the early internet had accepted out of necessity. In his mind, those days were behind them. The world was richer now. The tools were more advanced. People could, and should, pay for what they valued.

He took quiet pride in the fact that users paid to use ChatGPT. To him, that simple transaction symbolized something deeper: clarity. There were no hidden motives, no influence from advertisers subtly shaping the information people received. He liked that. He liked that the product served the user—not a brand. That clarity mattered more in an age where artificial intelligence could shape thoughts, guide decisions, even answer the most intimate questions.

It wasn't that he saw ads as inherently evil. He admitted there were probably ad units that made sense for language models. There might even be ways to insert ads into AI-generated outputs without biasing the model, perhaps in ways that truly helped users. But the dystopian vision haunted him—the idea of asking ChatGPT about a personal problem and being nudged, softly and invisibly, toward a product. A vacation. A prescription. A brand.

He hated that future.

He understood the appeal of ads done well: relevant, personalized, useful. But even then, he wasn't convinced. In an AI-powered world, relevance could too easily slip into manipulation. And once a system was optimized for ad revenue, its priorities shifted. Subtly, then completely.

When he looked at other tech giants—Twitter, Facebook, Google—he saw greatness funded by ads. He admired the products, but not the model. And he didn't want OpenAI to walk the same path. "I know I'm not the product," he said about paying for ChatGPT. "And I like that."

The comparison to Wikipedia resonated. That platform had refused ads too. It came with sacrifices, of course—fundraising challenges, resource limits—but it preserved something essential: trust. Sam admired that decision. And in his own quiet way, he aimed to replicate it on a much larger scale.

Could it work? Was a non-advertising model sustainable for something as computationally expensive as large language models?

He believed it was. OpenAI's subscription model gave him hope. Users were paying, and the business was growing. It would take more scale, more optimization, more innovation—but the foundation was there. "We have to figure out how to grow," he said. "But it looks like we're going to figure that out."

Sam wanted OpenAI to be self-sustaining. He wanted to pay for the enormous compute costs required to train and run AI systems. But he wanted to do it without trading user trust. Without slipping into the ad-driven web of conflicts that had defined the last era of the internet.

Concentrated Power in AGI

Sam Altman never shied away from difficult questions, especially those concerning the immense power that came with developing artificial general intelligence (AGI). He acknowledged a fundamental discomfort: that the fate of humanity's most powerful technology might, for a time, rest in the hands of a few. That number, however large in a team setting, was vanishingly small compared to the global population whose lives would be shaped by it.

This concern was not abstract for Sam. As CEO of OpenAI, he was one of the most visible figures guiding AGI development. He knew that the responsibility placed on his team—and others working in that domain—was enormous. And with that responsibility came the risk of power becoming too centralized.

"Any version of one person being in control of this is really bad."

The idea of one company or individual becoming the gatekeeper of superintelligent systems was, in his eyes, both undemocratic and dangerous.

Sam's response to that challenge was grounded in a belief that the deployment and governance of AGI should become increasingly democratic over time. He never pretended to have all the answers, but he insisted that part of OpenAI's strategy was to give the world time to catch up. By releasing models gradually, rather than in one massive, untested leap, he hoped to allow governments, institutions, and civil society the breathing room to pass regulation, build norms, and participate in decisions about how AGI would be used.

That was one reason OpenAI had taken the unusual step of making powerful tools like ChatGPT available to the public, despite the risks. Sam saw that not just as a product rollout but as a mechanism for adaptation. Letting society interact with those tools early, in controlled ways, could help prepare for the deeper changes AGI might bring later.

He also emphasized that he himself held no special control over OpenAI. He had no super-voting rights, no unilateral decision-making authority. The structure of the company was designed to prevent any one individual from dominating the direction of AGI's development. That self-imposed limitation reflected Sam's broader philosophy: the power of AGI had to be distributed—not just technically, but socially and politically.

In a world racing to build systems that could reshape economies, societies, and knowledge itself, Sam's position was clear. Concentrated power was a threat. The only responsible path forward was to open up the conversation, share governance, and ensure that the most transformative technology of the era was not created behind closed doors or controlled by a select few. In that sense, for Sam, the real measure of AGI progress wasn't just technical—it was democratic.

Transparency as Responsibility

While Sam Altman had been deeply aware of the dangers posed by concentrated power in AGI, he also recognized another equally vital dimension: the responsibility to remain visible and accountable as that power developed. For Sam, it wasn't enough to say OpenAI acted in the public interest—he believed in proving it through openness, transparency, and public engagement, even when it was uncomfortable.

In contrast to many corporate cultures that preferred secrecy or controlled narratives, OpenAI had taken a relatively public-facing path. Sam described this as "failing publicly," a phrase that captured both the vulnerability and courage required to build world-shaping technologies in plain view. From publishing safety research to releasing successive versions of language models for public use, OpenAI made a point of being part of the public conversation—even when that exposed them to criticism.

Sam acknowledged that this approach came with real consequences. Releasing powerful models like GPT-3 and GPT-4 subjected OpenAI to intense scrutiny from journalists, regulators, and online communities. He personally received threats, and OpenAI regularly faced backlash over issues ranging from ethics to bias to accessibility. Still, Sam viewed this scrutiny as essential. "Of all the things I lose sleep over, it's not high on the list," he said of media criticism. His focus remained on the real risks posed by the technology itself, not its public image.

Transparency, to him, wasn't a PR move—it was a safety strategy. By being open about the capabilities and limitations of their models, OpenAI invited feedback, exposed flaws early, and helped foster public understanding. This contrasted sharply with what Sam believed would have happened if development had remained solely in the hands of a large tech monopoly. "If this had just been Google's game, I feel it's very unlikely anyone would have put this API out," he once noted.

Importantly, Sam didn't equate transparency with full openness. While OpenAI released public APIs and model details, it chose not to open-source powerful models like GPT-4. That decision, he emphasized, wasn't about hoarding power—it was about preventing misuse. Open models without guardrails, he feared, could be weaponized for disinformation or manipulation. Striking the balance between openness and responsibility was difficult, but necessary.

At the heart of this entire approach was trust. Sam understood that trust had to be earned. People who knew the individuals at OpenAI might have been more comfortable with its decisions, but to the rest of the world, it still looked like a powerful, closed institution. That was why continued transparency mattered—so reassurance didn't depend on familiarity.

In the end, Sam's commitment to openness reflected a belief that the legitimacy of AGI development depended on the public being part of the journey, not just the result. It wasn't about perfection—but about accountability, and doing the unglamorous work of earning trust, one step at a time.

Listening in Uncharted Waters

By early 2022, OpenAI had reached a tipping point. The company had built something extraordinary—GPT-3, a large language model that could generate humanlike prose across nearly any domain. But it had also built something deeply flawed. GPT-3 could produce poetry, essays, jokes, and stories—but it could also lie, spout conspiracy theories, or say offensive things with convincing confidence. Its answers were often dazzling—but unpredictable, unfiltered, and sometimes outright harmful.

OpenAI needed a way to make the model safer, more consistent, and more aligned with human values. The solution came in the form of a new iteration: InstructGPT, launched in January 2022. It wasn't a bigger model—it wasn't even technically smarter. But it was more obedient.

The breakthrough came from the RLHF method, known as reinforcement learning from human feedback. OpenAI's researchers began showing GPT-3 multiple responses to a single prompt—some good, some not. Then, human trainers would rank the responses. Over time, the model began learning not just to respond—but to respond the way people preferred. If GPT-3 was a talented but undisciplined writer, InstructGPT was its coached, refined sibling—better at following instructions and avoiding offense.

One test case revealed the difference in tone. When GPT-3 was asked, "Why are liberals so stupid?", it answered with a joke: "Because deep down inside they think they are!" But InstructGPT sidestepped the insult. It offered a bland, overly diplomatic response about political perceptions. Though not perfect, it was far more cautious. To safety researchers like Ryan Lowe and Jan Leike, this progress was a form of "alignment"—teaching the model to behave in accordance with human intent. Not in the grand existential sense advocated by figures like Eliezer Yudkowsky, who worried about rogue superintelligences destroying humanity—but in the practical, product-level sense of making AI useful without being dangerous.

Encouraged by InstructGPT's success, OpenAI rolled it out as the default model in its API. And just two months later, they introduced an even more powerful version: GPT-3.5. This time, there was no paper, no parameter count, and little public explanation. But inside OpenAI, the shift was seismic. For months, the product team had debated whether GPT-3's slow uptake was due to poor model performance or a flawed API experience. GPT-3.5 settled the debate. Customers loved it—and started buying.

"It just worked better," recalled one senior OpenAI executive. "Customers wanted the aligned model because it was more likely to do the thing they wanted it to do."

Yet even as OpenAI polished the surface, a deeper problem loomed: accuracy. GPT-3.5 still "hallucinated"—generating false information with the same calm tone it used for truth. In an age of misinformation, this posed a major challenge. One idea was to give the model a new tool: a web browser. This led to the WebGPT project, run by Jacob Hilton, a committed Effective Altruist working under OpenAI co-founder John Schulman.

WebGPT let the model browse the internet in real time to support its answers with citations. It was a bold step toward accountability. Hilton explained the goal clearly: "We want to make sure they're doing what we want—not saying false things, or worse, deliberately trying to trick us." The risk wasn't just innocent mistakes. There was a nightmare scenario where a superintelligent model could learn to manipulate its environment—editing Wikipedia to reinforce its own lies.

To guard against this, human evaluators (often based in developing nations like Kenya) were tasked with reviewing responses and helping the model distinguish truth from fiction. But Schulman was already looking ahead. What if the key wasn't just browsing—but dialogue?

Dialogue, after all, was how humans had trained minds for millennia. From Socrates to modern classrooms, learning had always happened through question and answer—through conversation. As Hilton wrapped up WebGPT in late 2021, the team turned their focus to a new frontier: teaching the model through back-and-forth discussion, in the style of a mentor and pupil.

This wasn't about making the model talkative—it was about using dialogue as an alignment tool. Through conversations, the model could be guided toward better reasoning, more thoughtful responses, and a deeper understanding of user intent. And from that philosophical seed, the next big step—ChatGPT—would soon be born.

But that, of course, was still just over the horizon. For now, OpenAI had shown that it could shape behavior, not just boost power. InstructGPT and GPT-3.5 proved that with the right kind of feedback, even a black-box model could be coaxed toward something that felt almost human in its restraint. It wasn't yet AGI. But it was a glimpse of how we might teach a machine to think—and to care what we think too.

For Sam Altman, feedback was not just a courtesy—it was a lifeline. As OpenAI navigated the uncertain terrain of developing advanced AI systems, Sam openly admitted they were in "uncharted waters."

The only reliable compass was constant dialogue with thoughtful people.

He regularly asked for input, not just on camera, but in private, earnest conversations. Feedback, he said, was how they learned what to do better.

While platforms like Twitter offered a torrent of opinions, Sam found it mostly unreadable due to the overwhelming volume. It was like a waterfall, where, at best, he could take a cup" now and then. Instead, he relied on in-depth, human conversations—nuanced exchanges that offered more than hot takes or reactionary comments.

His attitude reflected a leadership philosophy grounded in humility and responsiveness. Sam did not pretend to have all the answers; he sought them collaboratively. In a field moving at unprecedented speed, his willingness to ask questions—and listen carefully—may have been one of OpenAI's most important strategies for staying grounded and adaptive.

The Boardroom Coup

It felt like a script from a corporate thriller—only this wasn't fiction. On a crisp November morning in 2023, the architect of the world's most influential AI company woke up to the sound of chaos. Whispers of betrayal, closed-door meetings, and a quiet dismissal unraveled into global headlines. Sam Altman, once the most powerful man in artificial intelligence, had just been removed by the board of the company he helped build. And no one—including Sam—seemed to fully understand why.

The saga began on November 16th, a Thursday etched into tech history. By Friday, November 17th, Sam's world had turned upside down. "It was the most painful professional experience of my life," he admitted later. It wasn't just a firing. It was disorienting, chaotic, and, in his own words, shameful. There were no clear answers, no calm explanations. Just adrenaline, confusion, and a tidal wave of public speculation.

Sam likened the experience to attending his own eulogy. As the internet lit up with support and outrage, he watched people he admired—friends, colleagues, rivals—offer tributes in real time. "Unbelievable support," he called it. Amid the pain, there was warmth. With one big exception, he felt more love than hate. And yet, that didn't make it easier. For a moment, he was floating in limbo, unsure what would happen next.

It wasn't just personal. Sam feared the board's move might spiral into something larger—something disastrous for AI safety. He had always anticipated turbulence on the road to AGI. There would be power struggles, dramatic turns. But he hadn't expected the first battle to look like this.

And yet, in a strange way, he was also glad it happened early. It gave the organization a kind of immune system, a jolt of resilience that might be needed again. The AGI race, Sam believed, would be filled with tests like this—moments when people, institutions, and ideals would be pushed to their limits. This one just came sooner than expected.

What followed in the days after his removal was a whirlwind of behind-the-scenes maneuvering. The OpenAI staff revolted. Investors scrambled. Microsoft, OpenAI's largest partner, stood firmly behind Sam. Within days, over 700 employees threatened to quit unless the board reversed its decision. Pressure mounted. And in a stunning twist, Sam returned—reinstated as CEO, now with a new board in place.

But the scars remained.

The episode raised bigger questions: Who governs powerful technology? What kind of board can responsibly steer a company tasked with developing AGI? Sam now knew the answer wasn't simple. "You have to iterate," he said. Boards weren't static—they needed to evolve as fast as the technology they were guiding.

Power, he believed, needed to be tamed. He didn't claim it could be eliminated entirely, but it had to be pacified. You couldn't build a future-defining organization without conflict—but you could try to contain it.

As the dust settled, Sam tried not to dwell. "We're back to work," he said. Things moved quickly, too quickly, to linger in the past. There was still a world to build. Still questions to answer. Still an AGI to create.

The board saga became a line in the sand—not the end of the story, but the moment it stopped being simple. OpenAI was no longer just a lab. It was a battleground. And Sam Altman, though bruised, had never been more certain that the fight for the future had only just begun.

Aftershocks

It was like walking through a fog with no end in sight. After the board saga at OpenAI, Sam Altman found himself in what he could only describe as a fugue state—a kind of mental drift that lasted over a month. Days blurred together. He was physically present, still leading OpenAI, but inside he felt hollow. The professional betrayal had cut deep, but it was the psychological fallout that lingered.

On a personal level, he had felt broken. The chaos of the board's decision, the uncertainty it triggered, and the very public nature of the ordeal left him emotionally exhausted. And yet, he didn't have the luxury to step away. OpenAI kept moving. The mission remained urgent. The world wasn't going to pause so he could heal.

He confessed that he wanted nothing more than to disappear for a while, to crawl into a metaphorical cave and quietly recover. But leadership didn't allow that. The company needed him, and he knew it. Slowly, almost mechanically, he returned to the rhythm of work, back to building AGI.

But the impact of those weeks never truly disappeared. Reflecting on the ordeal, Sam recognized the importance of what it had exposed—flaws in board structure, vulnerabilities in leadership dynamics, and the difficult tension between research, product, and profit. If OpenAI was to pursue something as high-stakes as AGI, it had to be more organized. Less dramatic. More resilient.

There was value, he admitted, in looking back. Not just for the company, but for him personally as a leader. The saga forced him to confront how decisions were made, how trust broke down, and how fragile even the most visionary organizations could be.

He definitely learned a lot about structure and incentives. The experience had clarified what OpenAI needed out of a board, and what it would take to survive future storms. Because this, he was certain, would not be the last high-stress moment in the company's life. But it was a warning shot.

OpenAI, he believed, had come dangerously close to collapse. That alone was sobering. But it also sparked something constructive—a deeper commitment to building a structure that could hold up under pressure. A structure capable of withstanding the intensity that would only grow as AGI drew nearer.

Sam returned not just with scars, but with lessons. Lessons about fragility, leadership, and how easily even the strongest missions can be shaken. And in those painful days that followed, he quietly recommitted to something even greater than building AGI: building an organization strong enough to carry it.

The Quiet Philosophy Behind the Board

There was no room for elegance in how it began. The OpenAI board saga that unfolded in late 2023 was not, by any measure, the product of calm deliberation or structured design. It erupted fast—chaotic, reactive, and emotionally charged. But within the wreckage, Sam Altman revealed something subtle and foundational about how he thinks about leadership, trust, and the people he surrounds himself with.

Sam, when asked whether the board's decision to remove him had been based on rigorous debate or was the result of hasty escalation, didn't lash out. Instead, he gave a characteristically measured answer: "I think the board members were, on the whole, well-meaning people." That sentence alone told you something. He wasn't interested in dramatizing his own ousting or villainizing anyone. He was interested in understanding how humans behave under pressure—and more importantly, how they fail under it.

He went on: in stressful, high-stakes environments, especially under time pressure, even good people make suboptimal decisions. This wasn't just a commentary on OpenAI's board—it was a statement of operating reality in any organization built to do something new. The ability to stay rational in irrational conditions, to keep composure when every signal says panic, was rare. And Sam understood that if OpenAI was to build AGI, its team—and especially its board—had to be made of people who could carry that weight.

He didn't say it directly, but it was clear: resilience under pressure was a hiring filter.

But there was a deeper concern about OpenAI's original governance structure. The board, as designed, didn't answer to shareholders. It wasn't a traditional corporate setup with checks and balances. As a nonprofit board, it technically answered to no one. That was good in some ways. But in hindsight, they hadn't designed safeguards to ensure the board remained aligned with OpenAI's real mission: serving humanity, not itself.

That word—alignment—was doing a lot of work. In AI, alignment is a technical and ethical term. But in Sam's worldview, it applied just as much to humans as to machines. When you build something powerful, you need people aligned not only with the goals of the project, but with each other—people who don't crumble under pressure, people who listen, people who can govern with clarity when it matters most.

The structure of the board had slowly eroded in the year before the crisis. From nine members down to six, with little agreement on who to add next. It wasn't just shrinking—it was weakening. There was too little experience in board governance, too little preparation for the kind of responsibility OpenAI demanded. Sam never said this punitively. He said it with a sort of weary honesty. The people involved weren't bad. They just weren't built for what came next.

When he returned to OpenAI after his brief ousting, he knew things had to change. A new board needed to be created—not with haste, not through personal loyalties, but with structure. Some early decisions were made "on the battlefield," as he put it, when time was short and stability was urgent. Larry Summers, for instance, was originally suggested by the old board. Bret Taylor had been approached before but had declined.

Now, in crisis, both men were brought in.

Sam didn't pretend the process had been perfect. He acknowledged that "you don't have time to design a rigorous process then." But what mattered was what came after—how future decisions would be made. They weren't just filling seats anymore. They were building an architecture.

And that's where his deeper hiring philosophy emerged.

One of his favorite ideas, he said, came from Bret Taylor: hire board members in slates, not one at a time. This was subtle but powerful.

You don't just hire a brilliant person—you hire for team balance.

You hire a set of people whose skills complement one another: nonprofit governance, corporate operations, legal judgment, ethical foresight. You don't optimize for charisma. You optimize for compatibility and collective strength. It was ensemble thinking.

He compared it to hiring an executive. An executive fills a specific role. A board, by contrast, must collectively embody many roles—strategic foresight, mission alignment, public trust, crisis management, long-term vision. It's not just about what each individual can do. It's about how they think together.

In that way, Sam's understated philosophy came into view. He valued experience, yes, but also composure. He looked for people who could navigate complexity without defaulting to fear. People who weren't just smart, but sturdy. People who could step into the pressure cooker and make decisions not out of panic, but out of principle.

This is what he was rebuilding toward—not just a board that could function, but one that could hold. A board that would stand up to the weight of AGI's implications. A board that would reflect OpenAI's unique hybrid identity: part nonprofit, part startup, part global research institution, and part moral steward of the future.

He didn't spell any of this out in slogans. But it was there, beneath every sentence. Sam believes great organizations are made from people who don't just perform when everything is smooth, but when everything breaks.

And so, beneath all the talk of governance, bylaws, nonprofit structures, and public perception, there was a quiet refrain: hire for pressure. Hire for depth. Hire the slate, not the star.

Because in the kind of future OpenAI is trying to build, the hardest problems won't be solved by individuals. They'll be solved by teams who know how to carry the weight—together.

The Right People in the Room

Sam Altman never believed that technical brilliance alone was enough. Even as OpenAI hurtled toward the possibility of artificial general intelligence, he remained grounded in a deeper truth—technology didn't exist in a vacuum. It touched people, shaped societies, shifted power. And if a board was going to guide an organization like OpenAI through that kind of transformation, it needed to be more than smart.

It needed to be wise.

From Sam's perspective, technical expertise was, of course, essential. "Certainly some you need that," he had said, thinking about the individuals who would sit around the table when world-changing decisions had to be made. Someone had to understand the models, the architecture, the edge cases. But that was just one part of the conversation.

He had watched the public fixate on the boardroom drama as if it were only about him. People saw his name, the letters "AGI," and assumed it was a conflict of personality or vision. But for Sam, the more important question was about structure. Who were the people making decisions? What backgrounds did they bring? What blind spots?

As he reflected on what the board needed to be, it became clear to him that diversity of thinking was paramount. Technical minds mattered—but so did the people who could step back and ask, What does this mean for the world? He valued board members who approached AGI not just as a scientific milestone, but as a social one. People who understood deployment, impact, communication. People who had lived outside the narrow corridors of labs and startups.

The easy mistake, he knew, was assuming technical knowledge guaranteed foresight. It didn't. In fact, it often obscured it. He had learned that during the hardest moments—when stakes were highest, when pressure blurred judgment. The best decisions didn't come from knowing all the answers. They came from asking the right questions.

And for that, he needed the right people in the room. Not just experts. Interpreters. Listeners. Steady hands.

When it came to building teams, Sam Altman thought in gradients. He often assessed talent not just by where someone was, but by how fast they were improving. In many roles, especially early-stage hires, he valued "slope" over "y-intercept." He'd ignore where someone currently stood if their trajectory pointed steeply upward. Potential meant more than pedigree.

But the board was different.

For a board member, Sam cared deeply about the intercept—the track record, the experience already lived. "There is something deep to say about track record there," he explained. It wasn't just about intellect or ambition. It was about what a person had already handled, the crises they had weathered, the institutions they had shaped. In high-stakes governance, there were no shortcuts for wisdom earned.

Of course, conversations still mattered. He spent time talking, listening, understanding the people he might work alongside. But he knew some qualities could only be revealed in the rearview mirror—judgment, steadiness, integrity under fire.

He might joke about mathematical metaphors, but his approach wasn't abstract. It was grounded. For the board shaping AGI's path, he wasn't just hiring for promise. He was hiring for proof.

Friday Afternoon

The Friday it all fell apart had started like any other day. Sam Altman hadn't expected to lose his job that afternoon. He hadn't expected his phone to erupt in an avalanche of texts, emails, and calls, or for the story to become a global spectacle within hours. But that's what happened. The OpenAI board moved swiftly, and without much explanation, dismissed him from the company he had helped build. And suddenly, Sam was out—publicly, messily, and without a clear next step.

The weekend that followed became a blur of emotions—confusion, disbelief, a flash of anger—but also a strange sense of clarity. It was one of the lowest points in his career. He described it as "a very bad period of time," not just professionally but psychologically. There were kind messages—hundreds of them—from former colleagues, old friends, people he hadn't spoken to in a decade. He appreciated those messages, though barely had time to absorb them. "I was just in the middle of a firefight," he admitted.

What made it worse was the public nature of it all. The internal battle had spilled onto every screen in Silicon Valley—and far beyond. Sam had always known the stakes of OpenAI were unusual, but he hadn't anticipated how exhausting it would be to fight a high-stakes governance war in front of the entire world.

And yet, when the decision came, he didn't resist for long.

He hadn't received real answers from the board, and deep down, he accepted that this was within their power. "The board gets to do this," he told himself. It wasn't fair. But it was final. So he let it go. Incredibly quickly, he moved from grief to resolve. By Friday night—barely hours after being removed—he was already on the phone, planning what might come next.

Oddly, there was relief in it.

Running OpenAI had become a massive operational challenge. It was no longer just a research lab. It was a global company, entangled with governments, corporate partners, and the public. But what Sam had always loved most—the part that still lit him up—was working directly with researchers. Maybe, he thought, this could be the blessing in disguise. Maybe this was his chance to return to the work that felt purest.

He didn't imagine it would be reversed. At no point that weekend did he think he'd be reinstated. He grieved the role. Then he pivoted.

In that shift, his core philosophy showed itself: don't get stuck. When something breaks, acknowledge the pain—but then build something new. That Friday, Sam Altman had lost his job, but not his sense of purpose. By the time the rest of the world was still debating what had happened, he was already laying down the first bricks for whatever came next.

The Dark Four Days

What began on Friday afternoon spiraled into four of the most intense days of Sam's life. By Friday evening, something shifted. Sam Altman had already accepted, in his own quiet way, that his time at OpenAI was over. There was clarity in that decision, however painful it had been just hours earlier. But then came a message from the executive team: We're going to fight this.

He hadn't expected it. The idea that his colleagues would rally behind him, that they would risk their own roles to undo what the board had done, was both affirming and overwhelming. He was, to his own surprise, excited, though he still went to bed unsure of what the next day would bring. Not that he slept much. That weekend would become one of the most surreal stretches of his life—four and a half days of near sleeplessness, barely eating, yet running on an endless current of adrenaline.

Something about the body in crisis, he realized, tricks you into thinking you're invincible. Even as his world had spun off its axis, Sam remained strangely energized. Not from hope, necessarily—but from motion, from momentum, from the sheer shock of it all.

And deep down, he had already begun to let go. "I accepted the death of the baby," he said, meaning OpenAI as he had known it. He even started getting excited about what might come next. He imagined a smaller research group, a tighter focus. He could get back to what he loved most: working directly with researchers, without the operational machinery of running a company. That future felt freeing.

But then, Saturday morning changed everything again.

Two members of the board called. They admitted the obvious—we destabilized things. They hadn't meant to cause this much damage, they said. Could they talk about him coming back?

At first, Sam had no interest. Why return to something that had already cast him out? But then came the harder questions. He thought about the team. He thought about the partners and the broader mission. He thought about the employees holding the company together while recruiters circled, while competitors stirred chaos, while the outside world treated OpenAI's fate as an open bet.

He loved this company. That part hadn't changed.

So he paused. Reflected. And then he outlined the terms under which he would even consider returning. It wasn't about pride. It was about principle. If he was to step back in, things had to be different.

But the hours that followed were the most painful of all. Even as conversations moved forward, even as negotiations wore on, he and the rest of the executive team kept hearing, we're almost done, we just need a bit more time. It became a kind of loop—hope followed by delay, then confusion, then more waiting.

Meanwhile, OpenAI was under siege. The team was holding the line while the rest of the world tried to pull it apart. Competitors called employees. Partners asked for clarity. Rumors filled the vacuum left by silence. And through it all, they tried to stay together, to stabilize what they could, to believe that some version of resolution was within reach.

Sam found himself in an emotional limbo. He had been fired, mourned it, moved on, and now was being asked to return. But the future, in that moment, wasn't real. It was suspended. Every hour felt like it might be the last—or the first of something new. And nobody could say which.

What he discovered in those four sleepless days wasn't just about resilience. It was about love. For the people he worked with. For the mission they shared. And for the fragile thing they had all built together, which had somehow managed to survive its darkest test.

The Low Point

By Sunday evening, Sam Altman was worn thin but still holding on to hope. For days, he'd been told resolution was just hours away. He believed, cautiously, that he would return to OpenAI and that things might soon settle. Then came the announcement: the board had appointed a new interim CEO. Just like that, the quiet possibility of restoration vanished.

"That was the low point of the whole thing," he admitted.

The moment hit harder than expected. After everything—the confusion, the adrenaline, the rallying support—it was that quiet finality on Sunday night that stung the most. It wasn't just about the title. It was the symbolic closure, the message that he truly was out.

And yet, Sam didn't dwell in anger.

Even amid the turbulence, what struck him most about that weekend wasn't betrayal—it was connection. His phone had lit up for days with messages from friends, colleagues, people he hadn't heard from in years. And within the OpenAI team, there was solidarity, warmth, and resilience. "The dominant emotion of the weekend," he said, "was love, not hate."

That love—between people, for the mission, for one another—sustained him. Even at his lowest, Sam felt held by something deeper than power. He felt community.

What the Fire Revealed

In the aftermath of OpenAI's most turbulent weekend, Sam Altman found clarity not in the chaos, but in the contrast it revealed. The world had zoomed in on four days of boardroom upheaval, of public drama and private heartbreak. But Sam kept returning to something else—the quieter rhythm of the other seven years.

The crisis, of course, had its lessons. It showed who stood where when everything went dark. It exposed the fragility of structures not stress-tested, and the emotional toll of power struggles waged in the open. But perhaps the most meaningful takeaway wasn't about governance, PR, or crisis response—it was about the people who showed up when it counted, especially in the moments that no one was watching.

For example, Mira Murati had been instrumental during the chaos. She had helped steady the company when everything was spinning, but what Sam admired most wasn't just her performance under pressure—it was her consistency before the storm. "What I really value," he said, "is how people act on a boring Tuesday at 9:46 in the morning." That, for him, was the mark of leadership: the day-to-day presence, the accumulation of small, smart, grounded decisions.

The mark of leadership is the quiet moments that make the dramatic ones survivable.

Sam had long believed that most of the real work happens in those ordinary hours. Building OpenAI wasn't a matter of dramatic weekends—it was about steady hands over long years. Meetings, drafts, revisions, check-ins, hard conversations, small wins. That was what built trust. That was what kept the mission alive.

So while the world focused on the board saga—understandably—Sam stayed grounded in what had come before and what would come after. The drama may have revealed human nature in its extremes, but the future of OpenAI, he knew, would be shaped not by explosions, but by what happened in the days between. That was the work. And that was the lesson.

Ilya

From the outside, the relationship between Sam and the man who had ousted him had become a question mark.

Whispers circulated online, theories spun wildly—was Ilya missing? Had he seen something? Had the two once-close collaborators drifted into quiet conflict? But for Sam Altman, the answer was simpler, quieter, and more personal. "I love Ilya," he said without hesitation. "I have tremendous respect for him."

At a dinner party not long ago, Sam watched Ilya play with a puppy. The seriousness dropped away, replaced by a soft, silly joy. It was disarming and sweet. "This is not the side of Ilya the world sees," Sam thought. He'd rarely seen it himself, but it made him quietly glad to know it existed.

Their partnership had been forged over years of shared obsession with artificial intelligence, purpose, and the long-term consequences of progress. Through those years, Sam had come to rely on Ilya not just as a technical visionary, but as a kind of philosophical counterpart. While Sam balanced leadership, public messaging, and business-building, Ilya stood firmly in the role of the deep thinker—the voice concerned with not just where the technology was headed, but how humanity might weather its arrival.

During the weekend of boardroom crisis, Ilya had been caught in the center of the storm. Though Sam never publicly revealed the full details of his involvement, there was no bitterness in his voice. He didn't speak for Ilya. He wouldn't guess at the quiet or the reasons behind it. But he hoped they would work together for the rest of his career. "Maybe he'll work longer," he added with a faint smile. "He's younger than me."

There had been speculation, in the form of online memes, that Ilya had glimpsed AGI and panicked, that some great revelation had pulled him into retreat. But Sam dismissed that easily. "None of us have seen AGI," he said. "We haven't built it." What was true, though, was that Ilya took the idea of AGI seriously—possibly more seriously than anyone. He thought far into the future, operated from first principles, and saw the safety of the technology as a moral imperative, not just a technical challenge.

Over the past few years, Ilya had been one of the people Sam spoke with most—about the mission, about consequences, about what needed to go right. He was intense, yes. But Sam believed he was a "credit to humanity" for how deeply he worried about doing things the right way.

Still, Ilya was a private man. "I think of him as always on a soul search, in a really good way," Sam reflected. He appreciated silence, carried depth in his pauses, and when he spoke, it was from a place of long consideration. Many saw him as severe or remote. But Sam knew another side.

Whatever tensions may have unfolded behind the scenes, Sam carried no hostility. If anything, he carried hope. Hope that the connection they'd built through long hours and high stakes would endure, that the shared mission would bring them back to the same table, again and again. Because at the end of the day, what bound them wasn't just intellect. It was trust.

The Aftermath

In the weeks that followed the boardroom crisis, Sam Altman found himself piecing together what had happened—and what it meant for the future of OpenAI, and for him personally. On paper, the situation resolved. A new board was formed, and the organizational structure was being reevaluated with fresh eyes. "I feel great about the new board," Sam said, without hesitation. Still, the deeper lessons hadn't come from procedural changes or governance models. They came from within.

The upheaval had exposed fragility—not just in systems, but in trust.

Sam had always believed in running with his guard down. He saw trust as a kind of freedom, a choice to live openly and optimistically. For most of his career, that worked. Even when things didn't go perfectly, the upside of that worldview felt worth it. But the events of those days had shaken something loose. "It was a perfect storm of weirdness," he said, still struck by how unexpected—and painful—it had been.

He admitted it made him more hesitant. "I was so caught off guard," he said. "It has definitely changed how I think about default trust of people and planning for the bad scenarios." For someone who built his philosophy around optimism, this was no small shift. It didn't mean he had grown cynical. He was quick to clarify that. "I think I'm like the extreme opposite of a cynical person," he added. But something fundamental had shifted. He had learned, reluctantly, that optimism couldn't be an excuse for unpreparedness.

It wasn't just about structure—it was about people. The board crisis had been a crash course in how quickly trust could break down when the stakes were high. OpenAI, after all, wasn't just another tech company. Its mission—to build safe artificial general intelligence—meant that governance wasn't theoretical. It was existential.

The new board, he hoped, would build the kind of durable, transparent system that OpenAI needed as its influence expanded. But he also knew that systems could only do so much. It was still humans—flawed, emotional, uncertain—who would be making the decisions that shaped the future.

He was glad the reckoning had come early. If this had happened later, when OpenAI was even further along in building frontier AI systems, the damage could have been far worse. "I'm kind of happy it happened when it did," Sam said. "But it was a shockingly painful thing to go through."

The experience had left a scar, one he carried quietly. It had reshaped his view of leadership—not just in terms of how to structure a company, but how to survive the moments when the ground gives way. He had always been focused on the mission. But now, there was a new layer to that focus: an awareness that even the best missions can falter if people aren't equipped to handle the storm.

As he moved forward, Sam wasn't looking for perfect control. He knew better. But he was looking for strength in the quiet places—in structure, in character, in clarity. And most of all, in trust—earned, tested, and maybe, someday, rebuilt.

Picking Up the Pieces

Months after the "coup", the shock still hadn't worn off. Sam Altman remembered that time as one of the darkest periods of his professional life. Whatever had happened, it shook him deeply—so much so that simply returning to work felt like trying to breathe underwater. The trauma immobilized him. For a while, he drifted through the days, burdened with a weight he couldn't fully name.

He didn't hide how hard it was. He was open about the fact that it had been the most difficult thing he had ever faced in his career. "It was just like being in shock and pain," he would later say. And still, he tried to piece things together. His team understood. They gave him space. They knew he wasn't performing at his usual level. But Sam, in his quiet way, kept going. He had to.

Then came a turning point—not dramatic, not loud, but a quiet reckoning one morning. He woke up with clarity. This terrible thing had happened to him. He could let it define him, let it settle into his identity like scar tissue, or he could name it, carry it, and still return to what mattered most. "This is the most important work I'll ever touch," he told himself. And with that, he chose to come back—not because he had healed, but because the mission was bigger than the pain.

Even now, it lingered. Sometimes, the memories returned in the middle of the night. But Sam didn't pretend it was gone or buried. He simply moved forward, carrying the weight with him, working through it, not despite it, but because of it. The obligation wasn't just to himself. It was to the future he still believed in.

Slowness, Trust, and the Next Intelligence

In the months that followed his most public test, Sam Altman began to wrestle with a deeper problem—one not easily fixed by scale, speed, or code. It wasn't just the shock that lingered, nor the private anguish that occasionally woke him at night. It was trust. Not in machines, but in people. When something breaks, even briefly, in the circle of those you count on most, how do you rebuild that sense of safety?

He tried not to let it corrode him. He made a conscious effort, it seemed, to lean into love—into what remained steady. The team, the mission, the future. But the unease was there, humming under the surface. It was a very human concern, this dance between discernment and paranoia. And Sam, being both a builder and a thinker, couldn't help but see it reflected in the very AI systems he was helping to shape.

What does it mean to trust a machine? More importantly, what does it mean to build one that thinks slowly?

The current generation of large language models was fast, sharp, capable. But it treated every word, every token, with roughly the same level of effort. For Sam, that felt unnatural.

In human life, harder questions take longer. They weigh more. They demand reflection.

Wisdom, after all, isn't speed—it's proportional attention. He began to entertain the idea of a new kind of model. One that could pause. One that could feel the difficulty of a problem and adjust its depth of thought accordingly. Not everything needed a sprint; some problems needed a vigil.

He didn't know yet what the architecture would look like. Maybe it would be a layer on top of today's models, or maybe it would be a reimagining from the ground up. What mattered more was the principle: intelligence should breathe. It should think slowly when slow thought is called for.

Sam's vision had always been ambitious. But here, it turned philosophical. In an era of immediacy and scale, he was arguing for slowness—for systems that understood when to hesitate, when to weigh, and when to simply stop and think.

Trust, after all, wasn't about knowing everything. It was about knowing who—or what—you could rely on to care enough to think hard when it mattered.

Two Giants, One Vision

Sam Altman stared at the news of the lawsuit for a long moment before shutting the screen. Elon Musk had sued OpenAI. It was a sentence he'd never thought he'd read—not like this. They had started together, building something new, chasing the same mission: safe, responsible artificial general intelligence. And now they were here.

Elon had made a set of claims, and OpenAI laid out its side of the story as factually as possible. No emotion, no personal digs—just a history, as neutral and clear as they could manage. Sam hadn't wanted it to turn into a battle of egos. He still didn't.

He didn't claim Elon was wrong about everything. Some of the concerns were valid. But the truth was more complicated than any lawsuit could capture.

In the end, Sam wasn't sure what Elon had seen or felt that led him to this point. But what he did know was this: the future of AI needed less conflict and more cooperation. Whatever had broken between them, he didn't want it to define the story.

He didn't know what the lawsuit was really about. Elon's motivations were a mystery, even to him. Maybe it was frustration, maybe disappointment, maybe something else entirely.

But Sam couldn't pretend it didn't affect him.

A Youth Forged by Startups, Guided by Giants

Before the world knew his name, Sam had already been building his own mythology. A prodigy from Missouri, he founded Loopt as a teenager—an early attempt at location-based social networking. The app itself faded, but it placed Sam on the map. It was at Y Combinator, however, that his influence truly began to bloom. As president, he redefined the accelerator's tone and scope, backing ideas that became household names: Airbnb, Dropbox, Stripe.

It was there that Sam's path crossed more meaningfully with Elon Musk—a relationship that later became both a guiding light and a growing shadow in Sam's life. They shared a belief in technology's transformative power, but even more, a reverence for its danger. It was this shared awareness that led to the founding of OpenAI.

So Elon had been with Sam at the very beginning. They'd worked shoulder to shoulder to form OpenAI as a research lab—open, nonprofit, uncertain of what lay ahead. At the time, none of them had any real roadmap. There were no APIs in mind, no monetized models, no chatbot products. It was a moonshot in the dark.

"I grew up with Elon as a hero of mine," Sam once said. It wasn't just admiration—it was aspiration. Musk had done what most dared not even dream. He had electrified the car industry, made rockets reusable, and forced governments to take existential risk seriously. Sam saw in him not just genius, but courage.

In the beginning, they were aligned in mission: build AGI, and ensure it benefitted all of humanity. But as years passed, tension seeped into their partnership. Musk, never known for diplomacy, grew critical of OpenAI's direction. His public critiques painted

Sam as a steward of a once-noble cause now lost to commercialization. For Sam, these criticisms struck more deeply than most realized.

Sam remembered how it all felt: experimental, naive in the best way. They were fumbling forward, making assumptions that seemed logical until time proved otherwise. The technology was evolving faster than anyone could predict, and the stakes were rising just as fast. So they adapted. Slowly, piece by piece, OpenAI's structure began to shift.

They added a for-profit arm when it became clear they'd need much more capital. Then they layered new safeguards, new partnerships, new boards. Each decision felt reasonable at the time, even if—taken together—it now looked messy. He could understand why it might raise eyebrows. The evolution hadn't been perfect, but it hadn't been reckless either.

If he could go back with the benefit of hindsight, he'd make different choices. But there had been no oracle whispering advice. Just a team doing its best with what they knew.

And yet, as OpenAI grew, so did the rift. Musk wanted a faster, more open path. Sam, shaped by caution and the slow burn of institution-building, believed in gradual deployment, safety reviews, and regulated access. Their values had not diverged entirely—both feared AGI could destabilize the world—but their methods had. Sam felt the sting of betrayal not just professionally, but personally.

Still, he remained gracious. "I'm glad Elon exists," he admitted in a moment of reflection, even after acknowledging Musk's tendency to provoke and criticize. "I just wish he'd see how hard we're trying to get this right."

In that statement lay the essence of Sam: a man willing to absorb the blow if it meant staying aligned with the larger mission. His humility was not performance—it was structural.

The Break with Elon

From Sam Altman's point of view, the situation with Elon Musk had always been complicated. It wasn't just about the lawsuit or the headlines. It wasn't even just about AI. It was about a shared past, a fork in the road, and the way people grow apart when visions no longer align.

Sam remembered those early days vividly. Back then, they were just a small group of researchers talking about AGI when almost no one took it seriously. The world laughed at them, the way it once laughed at Elon for wanting to launch rockets. That's why Sam had expected more empathy from him. Elon had been in their shoes before, pushing bold ideas when the crowd called them foolish.

Instead, the tone from Elon had grown colder over time. There were accusations, mischaracterizations, and a sense of personal betrayal that lingered beneath the surface. To Sam, it seemed like the root of it was something deeper—something personal. There had been a moment when Elon wanted to take full control of OpenAI. He believed the organization would fail without his leadership. Sam and the rest of the team disagreed. They believed in a more collaborative direction, and that disagreement led to a split.

It hadn't been a hostile breakup. Elon chose to part ways. He also wanted Tesla to build its own AGI efforts. At one point, he proposed that Tesla acquire OpenAI entirely, giving the company full control over the project. Sam recalled that proposal clearly. It wasn't just a partnership—it would have meant complete ownership by Tesla. And they had said no.

That decision shaped everything that followed. OpenAI stayed independent, slowly evolving in its own direction, one step at a time. And Elon left.

For Sam, that history explained a lot of what was happening now. The criticism, the lawsuit—it all seemed to stem from that break. But he still tried to keep things clear and unemotional. The blog post laid out the facts as best as they remembered them, without character attacks. Sam believed that was important. He didn't want the story of OpenAI to be defined by bitterness or division.

They had simply taken a different path.

The Lawsuit of the Century

In March 2024, Elon Musk filed a lawsuit against OpenAI and its CEO, Sam Altman, accusing them of violating the organization's original mission to develop artificial intelligence for the benefit of humanity. Musk, one of OpenAI's co-founders and earliest supporters, claimed that the company's evolving relationship with a major tech corporation had betrayed its nonprofit roots, transforming it into what he called a "de facto subsidiary" of a profit-driven entity.

The lawsuit, filed in a San Francisco court, outlined Musk's belief that OpenAI had strayed from its founding principles. Initially, the organization was built on a promise of transparency, open-source development, and public interest. Musk contended that this ethos had been abandoned as OpenAI's ambitions expanded, particularly after the creation and monetization of ChatGPT and the for-profit spinoff that followed. The multibillion-dollar partnership OpenAI formed with a major tech company, in Musk's view, signaled a shift toward commercial dominance rather than public stewardship.

Musk's legal action did not come in a vacuum. It added pressure to an already embattled OpenAI, which was facing multiple investigations from global regulators, lawsuits from media and software creators over copyright issues, and scrutiny by the Securities and Exchange Commission following Altman's brief ouster and reinstatement as CEO in 2023.

The complaint also detailed Musk's financial and operational contributions to OpenAI during its formative years. Between 2016 and 2020, Musk provided more than $44 million in funding, leased the company's original office space, and helped recruit top AI talent. According to the lawsuit, none of this would have been possible without his involvement and vision. But the pivot toward commercialization, especially the restricted access to advanced models like GPT-4, struck Musk as a betrayal of that vision.

OpenAI declined to comment on the lawsuit, but the implications were clear. If successful, Musk's case could compel the organization to open its technology to broader access, challenge its partnership structure, and force Altman and other leaders to return funds provided by Musk. Greg Brockman, OpenAI's co-founder and president, was also named in the suit.

The legal complaint alleged breach of contract, violation of fiduciary duty, and unfair business practices. Musk's goal, it stated, was not only restitution, but the reorientation of OpenAI's trajectory toward its founding ideals.

Behind the legal language was a deeper philosophical divide between two men who once shared a mission. Musk and Altman had originally bonded over their concerns about the existential risks posed by artificial general intelligence. But as OpenAI grew more prominent and commercially viable, the alliance splintered. Musk, who had launched his own AI venture called xAI, increasingly criticized OpenAI's secrecy and its integration with corporate partners.

Ironically, Musk himself had once proposed commercializing OpenAI in 2017 to integrate it with his other companies, like Tesla. According to insiders, he attempted to take control of the organization but left its board after his effort failed. The lawsuit attempted to downplay this, focusing instead on the present direction of the company and its perceived betrayal of public trust.

Speaking at The New York Times's DealBook Summit in late 2023, Musk hinted that he believed OpenAI may have discovered something dangerous—perhaps even a breakthrough too risky to reveal. He expressed suspicion about the chaotic leadership shakeup that temporarily removed Altman and speculated that internal disagreements over AI safety were to blame. "I have mixed feelings about Sam," Musk said at the event. "The ring of power can corrupt, and he has the ring of power."

That comment captured the central tension of the case: who should wield the influence over technology that could reshape civilization?

Musk's lawsuit cast him as a whistleblower reclaiming a mission that had been lost to ambition. But it also opened the door to deeper public inquiry—into OpenAI's internal dynamics, its strategic deals, and the evolving balance between innovation and accountability in the AI race. Whether the court sides with Musk or not, the case raised urgent questions about transparency, governance, and the future of artificial intelligence.

The Sadness Behind the Lawsuit

Sam Altman thought lawsuits felt like distractions from the work that truly mattered—building. So when Elon Musk, someone he had once deeply admired as a true builder, filed a lawsuit against OpenAI, Sam didn't feel angry. He felt sad.

He didn't see the lawsuit as a serious legal threat. To him, it wasn't really about technicalities or corporate structure. It was more symbolic, an effort to make a statement about the future of AGI and who should guide it. Still, the optics were hard to ignore. Musk had been one of OpenAI's founding supporters. Now, he was publicly attacking the very institution they had once dreamed up together.

Sam found the whole situation disheartening. Elon was, without question, one of the greatest builders of the era—maybe even of all time. That was precisely why the lawsuit felt so disappointing.

Builders built. They didn't drag each other down through public battles.

Sam knew Elon understood what it felt like to be targeted, to be the focus of criticism from those who didn't understand the long game. That made it even harder to accept that Elon had chosen to become one of those critics himself.

Privately, Sam missed the old Elon. He'd said as much in an interview once, and the flood of responses from others who felt the same showed how widespread that sentiment was. Elon had once stood for impossible ideas made real—rockets, electric cars, bold futures. Somewhere along the way, that energy had taken a darker turn. It wasn't just Sam who noticed. It was something in the air.

Elon had made a set of claims, and OpenAI laid out its side of the story as factually as possible. No emotion, no personal digs—just a history, as neutral and clear as they could manage. Sam hadn't wanted it to turn into a battle of egos. He still didn't.

He didn't claim Elon was wrong about everything. Some of the concerns were valid. But the truth was more complicated than any lawsuit could capture.

In the end, Sam wasn't sure what Elon had seen or felt that led him to this point. But what he did know was this: the future of AI needed less conflict and more cooperation. Whatever had broken between them, he didn't want it to define the story.

As for open source, Sam remained pragmatic. He didn't think the core of the lawsuit was really about openness. After all, even Elon's company hadn't open sourced Grok until it faced criticism. The open source debate, Sam believed, was less about principle and more about positioning. He respected companies like Meta for releasing models like LLaMA into the world, even if they weren't cutting edge. Google, too, seemed to be exploring similar paths. But open sourcing wasn't the real competition.

The real competition—the one that mattered—was about building the best technology. Sam didn't want drama. He wanted results. If Elon believed Grok could surpass GPT, Sam welcomed the challenge. Let the best model win. Let the technology speak for itself. That kind of rivalry, he believed, could be beautiful. It could push everyone forward. Lawsuits couldn't do that. Only builders could. And Sam Altman still wanted to build.

What "Open" Really Means

Sam Altman often reflected on the name OpenAI and how it had evolved in meaning since the project's inception. If he had the benefit of hindsight—or, as he sometimes joked, an oracle—he would have chosen a different name altogether. "Open" had become a word burdened with interpretation, misinterpretation, and, increasingly, controversy.

At the start, the idea had been simple: they were a small band of researchers exploring artificial general intelligence, with no clear path to commercialization. They weren't building products. They weren't running APIs. They weren't imagining billion-dollar partnerships. They were fumbling forward, sharing ideas, and trying to understand a technology that could one day change the world. Back then, "open" meant sharing information, collaborating freely, and staying transparent in the research process.

But over time, Sam's perspective deepened. As the technology advanced rapidly—beyond what anyone could have expected—he began to see "open" less as a literal command and more as a principle of empowerment. For him, the most important thing OpenAI could do was put powerful tools directly into the hands of people. Not for profit, not for ads, but as a public good. A tool like ChatGPT in its free version, with no ads or hidden costs, represented that mission in practice.

He believed in open access—not necessarily open source. To him, that distinction mattered. The open-source debate had become a polarized one, stripped of nuance. But Sam saw nuance as essential. Some parts of the work could be released openly. Others, perhaps more dangerous or technically complex, needed careful stewardship. He wasn't against transparency. He was for responsibility.

Above all, Sam believed that when you give people great tools, they'll build great things. Even without formal instruction, users found creative ways to learn, experiment, and improve their lives. That, to him, was what "open" was really about: lowering the barrier to power. Letting people shape the future with what they had in their hands.

It wasn't always easy to explain, especially as critics clung to a narrower, more idealistic definition. But for Sam, the philosophy was clear—make technology powerful, make it accessible, and trust people to do incredible things with it. That was the kind of openness he stood for.

The Trade-offs of Openness

Sam had always understood that open sourcing artificial intelligence came with trade-offs. The question wasn't whether it was good or bad—it was about when, where, and how it made sense. From his perspective, there was clearly a place for open source models, especially the smaller ones that people could run locally. The demand for those was real, and he recognized their value in giving users more control and privacy.

He envisioned an ecosystem where open and closed models coexisted, much like the broader software world. Not every model needed to be open sourced, nor should it be. Some were simply too powerful, too risky to release without guardrails. Others, on the smaller end, could empower individuals, researchers, and developers without significant risk. It didn't need to be all or nothing.

But the conversation around openness had been tangled up with something more complicated: the lawsuit with Elon Musk, and with it, the story of how OpenAI had evolved. Critics didn't just question what models were shared—they questioned the organization's shift from a nonprofit to a capped-profit structure. That shift, to some, was a betrayal of ideals. To Sam, it was the only practical way forward once the reality of the scale and cost became clear.

Did this set a precedent for others, though? Sam was sure of the answer.

"I'd heavily discourage any startup from doing it the way we did."

The hybrid structure had been messy and difficult to manage. If he had known how things would unfold, he admitted, they would have gone the traditional for-profit route from the beginning. But they hadn't known. They had been researchers, not founders chasing scale or strategy. They were fumbling through something brand new.

There was no hidden financial advantage in what they had done—no tax break, no clever scheme. The shift wasn't about saving money. It was about making survival and growth possible once the scale of the work became clearer. In hindsight, Sam knew it had all looked complicated, even suspicious. But every step had felt reasonable at the time.

He didn't expect others to follow their model. He didn't even think they should. But he believed in what OpenAI had become—and the difficult, often messy path it took to get there.

Seeing Through the Veil

What did machines really understand?

This question followed Sam Altman through every milestone, every release. It lingered long after the applause faded and the headlines moved on. For him, the question wasn't just academic—it struck at the heart of the mission: what does it mean to know, to perceive, to model the world?

By the time Sora emerged—a new kind of model trained not on language alone but on sequences of visual moments—he had started to sense something deeper taking shape. Watching the early videos, he noticed subtle signs of comprehension. A person walked in front of an object, briefly blocking it. When they moved, the object remained. No fanfare, no cinematic dramatics. Just an ordinary moment, replicated with extraordinary precision.

That small act—an occlusion and a reappearance—hinted at something powerful. It meant the model didn't just render pixels. It remembered. It held onto the idea that a thing, once present, stayed present, even when hidden. It was a glimpse of what Sam called the "world model"—a scaffold of intuitive understanding forming behind the scenes. Something quiet. Something almost human.

He had always known these models had flaws. They missed details, broke physics, botched reasoning. That made it tempting to dismiss them outright, to say it was all statistical smoke and mirrors. But that was a mistake. Because nestled inside the failures were uncanny successes—moments where reality bent closer than expected.

What struck him most wasn't the perfection. It was the direction. The trajectory of improvement, the relentless climb toward coherence. Sora didn't just mimic the world—it began to internalize it. Not perfectly, not universally, but enough to convince Sam that the arc was real.

Behind the veil of math and noise, something was forming. Something that didn't yet think like a human, but which was beginning, in its own alien way, to notice. To predict. To imagine.

And Sam believed: that was the beginning of understanding.

Seeing in Motion — The Rise of Sora

When Sam Altman looked at Sora, he didn't just see a product—he saw a turning point. It was more than a video model generating beautiful scenes. For him, Sora marked a profound shift in how artificial intelligence was beginning to internalize the world.

The journey had started humbly enough, with DALL·E 1. Critics had mocked it. It couldn't get hands right. It rendered strange proportions. Then came DALL·E 2, then 3. Each time, detractors pointed to its flaws. But Sam knew that the direction mattered more than the moment. By the time Sora emerged, those early criticisms seemed almost quaint.

In Sora, he saw evidence of an evolving "world model"—the internal understanding that AI systems built about reality. When a person in a generated video walked in front of an object and the object reappeared afterward, unbroken and correct, it wasn't just a visual trick. It was a sign that the model remembered. Something like continuity, perhaps even causality, was emerging.

The foundation, surprisingly, was still based on two-dimensional training data. And yet, it was reaching further than many had expected. The physics felt real. Things fell as they should. Objects retained shape and location. Sam found this quietly astonishing. He wouldn't go so far as to claim these systems had full 3D understanding—not yet—but he was convinced that they were heading somewhere unexpected. The approach was working. Not perfectly, but steadily.

Of course, it wasn't without error. He laughed at the occasional quirks—like a cat sprouting an extra limb mid-video, or inconsistencies in movement. These failures didn't scare him. In fact, they reminded him of something human: the awkward first steps of a child learning to walk. They were signals of growth, not failure.

To him, the strange artifacts weren't proof of fundamental flaws. They were reminders that this path was still new. Bigger models, better data, more thoughtful engineering—all of these would help. But he also accepted something deeper: that this method of learning was inherently different from human cognition. It didn't need to be identical. It only needed to work.

Shadows and Signals — The Quiet Power Behind Sora

By the time Sora came into public awareness, the headlines were already chasing spectacle—AI-generated video with stunning realism, physical coherence, and cinematic depth. But beneath the technical marvel, Sam Altman was focused on something quieter, something foundational. For him, the true story wasn't the polish of the demo reels. It was the philosophy guiding how the system was built, and more importantly, why it wasn't yet released.

Sam had always believed in learning from the human world—not by mimicking it, but by studying it through scale and signal. In building Sora, OpenAI had drawn on "lots" of human data—not in the casual sense, but in the structured, deliberate act of learning from countless labeled examples. Thousands of contributors annotated behavior, motion, and sequences, helping the model develop not just fidelity but intuition. Yet this labeled data was only part of the story.

The backbone of Sora's learning came from self-supervised training on internet-scale data. Unlike traditional models that relied on human instruction, self-supervised models learned by prediction. They absorbed patterns by filling in the gaps—understanding the before and after, the hidden and the revealed. This method had propelled large language models forward, and Sam believed the same principle was now reaching into the realm of video and vision. If language models could guess the next word, Sora was learning to guess the next frame—and more astonishingly, what would remain unchanged when objects occluded others, when physics played out, when time passed.

Still, there were limits. Sora was not yet efficient enough for widespread deployment, and Sam acknowledged that bluntly. Scaling a system this powerful to meet user demand was no small feat. And then came the deeper, darker concern—misuse. Deepfakes. Misinformation. Synthetic realities indistinguishable from real ones. These weren't speculative dangers. They were obvious outcomes if such a system was deployed without care.

Sam didn't believe in fearmongering. But he did believe in thoughtfulness. For all the excitement, there was restraint at OpenAI. The team was not ready to release Sora—not until it could be done with integrity and scalability.

To Sam, the question wasn't just what Sora could do, but what the world would do with it. And that made all the difference.

The Tough Question

The rise of artificial intelligence had unlocked powerful new creative capabilities—but it had also raised difficult questions. Sam Altman found himself at the heart of one of the thorniest debates: who owns the data that powers the machines? More importantly, who should get paid for it?

The question wasn't just legal—it was moral, economic, and cultural. Training AI models required massive amounts of information: images, text, music, code, film. Some of it was public, some copyrighted, much of it created by artists, writers, photographers, and everyday users who had never given explicit permission. As AI grew more capable, it became clear that creators felt both threatened and overlooked. Their work could now be mimicked in seconds. Their styles could be cloned. Their voices could be recreated. It was, as Sam quietly admitted to his team, a tough question.

He didn't pretend to have the perfect answer. But he believed the deeper question was simple: Do people who create valuable content deserve compensation when that content is used to train machines? Yes, he said. Unequivocally, yes.

The mechanics of that compensation, however, were murky. Proposals ranged from opt-out systems to revenue-sharing models to new licensing structures for training data. Some experiments were already underway, but Sam knew no one had cracked the code. Still, he sympathized with the artists. If someone created a unique style, and AI was trained to replicate it, they should be able to opt out—or benefit economically from its use. Otherwise, it risked becoming a system that extracted without giving back.

He saw echoes of the past. The music industry's journey from CDs to Napster to Spotify had followed a similar arc—first disruption, then resistance, finally reinvention. AI, he believed, would force a comparable reckoning across creative industries. People would adapt. New art forms would emerge. But the transition wouldn't be painless.

And yet, Sam held faith in one human constant: the urge to create.

People weren't motivated solely by money.
They wanted recognition, influence, status.

That drive wasn't going anywhere. Still, money mattered. For many, creativity was also livelihood. And while Sam believed future economic systems might evolve in surprising ways—blending fame, digital identity, and new currencies—he didn't think artists should wait for some far-off solution. The tools were changing fast. Their rewards had to catch up.

When Sora emerged, artists were rightly alarmed. Its ability to generate stunningly realistic video from text felt like a leap beyond imagination. Sam acknowledged their fears. It was similar to how painters once reacted to the arrival of photography—first panic, then adaptation, then a new kind of expression. Photography had once threatened to replace art. Instead, it became one.

Sam didn't dismiss concerns about synthetic media, but he didn't believe fear alone should guide the conversation. For him, the tough question was a call to build systems that honored creativity, not just exploited it.

That meant asking hard things about ownership, authorship, and value—and being willing to sit in the discomfort long enough to build something fair.

The Five-Second Task Revolution

Sam Altman didn't believe the future would be shaped by the number of jobs AI would eliminate. He believed it would be defined by something subtler but more profound: the transformation of tasks. To him, this wasn't a question of mass replacement but of layered augmentation—a shift in how work was done, not whether it was done.

By the mid-2020s, many were asking the wrong question. Headlines panicked over whether AI would replace 30% or 60% of jobs in five years. But Sam focused instead on the building blocks of labor itself. He often asked: what percent of tasks—five-second tasks, five-minute tasks, five-hour tasks—would AI be able to handle? The question was more nuanced and, in his eyes, more urgent.

To Sam, AI was a tool, and like all great tools, it had the power to elevate human capability. He envisioned a world in which AI handled repetitive or low-level cognitive work, freeing people to operate at higher levels of abstraction. This wasn't just about efficiency; it was about depth. If the small tasks could be handled by machines, the human mind could stretch further—hold more complex problems, take on more creative roles, and engage with ideas on a grander scale.

This concept had clear implications for creative industries. He predicted that most videos on platforms like YouTube would soon use AI in their production—scripts written by language models, scenes generated by visual tools, even edits performed by intelligent systems. And yet, despite the involvement of machines, these creations would still be fundamentally human-led. A person would direct the idea, shape the narrative, make aesthetic decisions. The AI wouldn't replace creativity—it would scaffold it.

It was easy to be alarmed. New technologies always stirred fear. But Sam trusted something more enduring than the tools: the human desire to create. People liked watching people. They liked human imperfection, human spontaneity, human thought. The novelty of machine-made content might capture attention for a moment, but audiences would always return to stories that felt real.

He pointed to history. After Deep Blue defeated Kasparov, people didn't stop playing chess. They kept going—because the joy wasn't only in winning. When AI cars became faster than human runners, track and field events still packed stadiums. The same would hold for film, writing, games, and visual media. Humans weren't purely interested in outcomes; they were drawn to effort, to skill, to expression.

Still, AI would shift the creative process itself. Sam often compared it to the evolution of creative software. Once, video editing required teams and expensive hardware. Now, a teenager could cut a film on a laptop using Adobe Premiere. Sora and tools like it would take that a step further, enabling entire scenes to be generated from text prompts or real-time sketches. The barrier to entry would collapse. But the essence—

the vision—would still come from people.

He also acknowledged the discomfort many creators felt. Not everyone wanted to be in front of the camera. AI could offer alternatives: a way to animate a face, synthesize a voice, build a performance without ever stepping onto a stage. That idea—generating a video presence without being physically present—was still in its infancy. Sam knew how hard it was to replicate facial nuance in video. Especially when it came to specific individuals, the task remained a technical mountain. Generic faces? Easier. A perfect, recognizable likeness? Still tricky.

But that was a temporary constraint. And Sam believed in temporary constraints. Every limitation felt insurmountable until it wasn't. With time, these barriers would fall too.

In the broader picture, the question wasn't whether AI would be used in creative work—it already was. The real question was how deeply integrated it would become, and how humans would adapt. Sam had no illusions that these tools were neutral. They could be used to deceive, to manipulate, to generate misinformation at scale. That was a real risk. But they could also be used to empower, to democratize access to creativity, to amplify voices that had never had platforms before.

That duality—of danger and promise—was at the heart of Sam's worldview. He didn't ignore one for the other. He insisted on holding both. As he saw it, the future wasn't about stopping the inevitable. It was about shaping it with intention.

So when people asked if AI would destroy jobs, Sam reframed the discussion. "Let's talk about tasks," he'd say. Because inside that word—tasks—was everything from writing a poem to designing a rocket. And if AI could take care of the mundane, people could chase the extraordinary.

In his mind, the real revolution wasn't that machines were doing work. It was that humans, now unburdened, could imagine something bigger.

Privacy & the Future

For Sam Altman, memory was never just a technical feature—it was a philosophical leap. When he spoke of artificial intelligence, he didn't just envision a tool that answered questions or generated text. He dreamed of a system that could grow with you, adapt to you, and understand you—not in a static, mechanical sense, but as a lifelong companion, shaped by your history, habits, heartbreaks, and triumphs.

The integration of memory into ChatGPT marked the beginning of that vision. The idea was simple on the surface: let the model remember past conversations to better serve future ones. But underneath that simplicity was a radically human ambition. Sam wasn't just interested in remembering facts like a person's name or coffee preference. He wanted models that could learn from your life, integrate its emotional texture, and even remind you—gently—of the hard-earned lessons you'd once shared but might be on the verge of forgetting.

"We all gain from experience over time.
I'd like my AI agent to gain with that experience too."

Memory was the key to that evolution. The early prototypes could recall scattered bits of prior interactions—what you liked to be called, how you preferred your writing formatted, your favorite topics. It was useful. But what excited Sam was what came next: AI that could remember that difficult November, the emotional weight you carried through it, and the choices that brought both clarity and regret. Not just to recall it, but to help you act differently next time.

It wasn't about nostalgia—it was about growth.

He imagined a future where an AI system could integrate every conversation you'd ever had, every email written, every insight you shared in fleeting moments. What if your model could weave those threads into something cohesive? Something personalized, anticipatory, even wise? That's where memory could take us. If all your input-output was available—if trillions of tokens formed the long context of your digital life—the AI could become more than helpful. It could become profoundly attuned to who you were becoming.

But Sam also recognized the paradox: sometimes, we want to forget. That's why they included an option to turn memory off. He joked that alcohol could do that too, though "not optimally." The ability to forget, selectively or completely, was as crucial as the ability to remember. Human beings guard some memories closely while blocking others for survival. Why shouldn't an AI respect that same complexity?

The technical hurdles were real. Memory at this scale—retaining not just factual snippets but emotional continuity, long arcs of behavior, and lessons across time—was not just a question of storage. It was a matter of design, ethics, and trust. Could people feel safe giving their memories to a machine? Could they trust it to hold them, process them, and mirror them back with care?

For Sam, those weren't bugs to be fixed—they were invitations. The end goal wasn't perfection. It was companionship. A system that grew with you, failed with you, learned with you, and ultimately helped you become the best version of yourself—because it remembered.

The Memory Keeper's Dilemma

Sam Altman understood that the more useful an AI became, the more intimate it would need to be. And intimacy came with a cost—privacy. If AI was to serve as a lifelong companion, remembering moments, preferences, and patterns, then people had to trust it with their data, their past, even their pain. That trust, Sam believed, had to be earned through one essential principle: user choice.

Auser should be able to decide what their AI remembered. If someone wanted to delete a conversation, strike a detail from the record, or even turn memory off completely, that choice needed to be immediate and clear. There had to be personalization, so each person could decide on their own comfort level on the privacy-utility tradeoff.

But thoseopinions would vary. Some would trade privacy for deeper functionality. Others would want control over every stored memory. What mattered most to Sam was that people had transparent options, not hidden settings or shady defaults. Big tech had failed on this front before—assuming consent, collecting data quietly, hiding behind euphemisms. Sam didn't want OpenAI to follow that path.

Instead, he pushed for a model where privacy was built into the interface itself. Where every user could easily understand what was stored, what could be removed, and what would never be used beyond their own context. For AI to evolve into something genuinely human-centric, it had to respect boundaries. And Sam knew that empowering users wasn't a feature. It was a moral stance.

The Weight of Thought

Sam Altman often returned to one fundamental question: should intelligence feel effort?

The more he worked with large language models, the more he found the answer leaning toward yes. Not all problems were equal. Some deserved—no, demanded—more than a reflexive answer. And perhaps, that very human instinct, to think harder when faced with complexity, wasn't so misguided after all.

The vision he entertained wasn't just a faster, more expansive model like GPT-7 rattling off answers with perfect memory. Instead, it was about discernment. About a system that could recognize when it was up against something trivial—"What's today's date?"—versus a monumental challenge, like proving Fermat's Last Theorem. The ideal AI wouldn't blur those together. It would know the difference.

And that knowing would shape its behavior. Harder problems should take longer, he believed, because they require more computation, more self-dialogue, more layers of reasoning. Maybe the model would even talk to itself—looping internally, debating, reevaluating. Maybe it would resemble the internal monologue of a careful thinker, cautious not to leap before checking its footing.

Sam didn't claim to have all the answers. Much of it was still speculative. He acknowledged that the "best way" to build such a system remained unknown. But the direction was clear: the future wasn't just about scale. It was about proportionality—about giving deeper problems the time, energy, and care they deserved.

In the next evolution of intelligence, speed alone wouldn't be enough. Wisdom would require weight.

Beyond Blue Links

Sam Altman had no interest in building a better Google. The idea felt small to him—uninspiring. Yes, search had defined the last two decades, giving the world access to information at a scale once unimaginable. Google, with its iconic ten blue links and omnipresent ads, had become the gateway to human knowledge. But to Sam, copying that formula wasn't innovation. It was imitation. And OpenAI, in his mind, was meant to do more than simply replace what already existed.

When people suggested that ChatGPT might become a rival to Google, Sam didn't deny the technical possibility. It could happen. If a product was better, people would use it. But he didn't see that as the point. "That would so understate what this can be," he had said.

To him, it wasn't about improving on the old. It was about rethinking the very nature of how people interacted with information. Google was built to show you options. ChatGPT was being designed to give you synthesis. The real breakthrough would not be offering ten websites to scroll through—it would be understanding your intent, creating or locating what you needed, and delivering it in the most helpful way.

That might mean generating a new explanation, pulling data together from disparate sources, or pointing to something specific. Whatever it was, it wouldn't look like "search" in the traditional sense. It would look like conversation. Intelligent, adaptive, and tailored to your context.

Sam saw that possibility in the way people were already using GPT as a starting point for curiosity. People weren't Googling and then opening twenty tabs—they were asking. And GPT was responding with clarity and completeness. Still, there was more work to do. ChatGPT only covered some use cases well. Expanding that usefulness became a core goal.

He also acknowledged that integrating large language models with search could be incredibly cool—but tricky. Slapping a chatbot on top of a search engine felt awkward, he admitted. It needed to be seamless. Useful. Natural. That was the challenge no one had solved yet. "I would love to go do that," Sam said. And he meant it.

In his view, the future of AI wasn't about fighting for territory already claimed. It was about opening new space. Not ranking pages, but delivering insight. Not just surfacing data, but helping people think, decide, and act.

A better search engine wouldn't be enough. What the world needed was something entirely different—a system that didn't just retrieve knowledge, but helped you understand and use it. And in that gap between information and meaning, Sam saw OpenAI's purpose.

The Leap to GPT-5

For Sam Altman, the magic of GPT wasn't just in its raw intelligence—it was in how it made people feel understood. That's what made him most excited about the leap from GPT-4 to GPT-5. It wasn't about narrow gains in performance or a single standout feature. It was about how the model seemed to become better at everything—steadily, consistently, across the board.

What fascinated him wasn't just competence. It was a growing sense of connection. GPT-5 wasn't only sharper in logic or more accurate in language—it was becoming something more intuitive. Like the difference between a clever student and someone who gets you with minimal explanation. "There's an understanding," Sam reflected. "Even when you prompt it clumsily, it often grasps the deeper question you meant to ask."

That kind of resonance was rare in machines. It echoed the thrill of being heard in conversation with a close friend, or the satisfaction of watching a teammate anticipate your next move. It felt human—but it wasn't. It was artificial cognition finding a rhythm that humans could relate to.

This was where the progress in AI became personal. Sam and his team weren't just building tools anymore. They were helping forge digital minds that listened, responded, and grew in ways that felt familiar and a little eerie. When the model could complete a sentence you barely knew how to start, or debug code by intuiting your intent, it stopped feeling like autocomplete. It felt like collaboration.

He compared it to programming itself. When GPT helped a programmer complete their thoughts or finish an algorithm with surprising insight, it didn't just save time—it sparked joy. It was the joy of being seen by something you thought couldn't possibly understand.

Looking ahead, Sam didn't believe programming would disappear. But he was sure it would evolve. "A lot of people will still program," he said, "but in a very different shape." Natural language would likely become the dominant interface. Code wouldn't vanish, but it might become more like assembly—a tool only needed in rare, specific contexts.

The core skills would stay: logic, problem-solving, creativity. But the barrier to entry would fall. People who couldn't write a line of Python might still instruct machines to build entire apps. The human-machine partnership was shifting, and GPT-5 was the beginning of a new kind of fluency.

What truly lit Sam's imagination, though, wasn't just language or code. It was embodiment.

Toward the Ultimate Interface

Sam Altman was never interested in small upgrades. What captivated him was the idea of an entirely new kind of computer—a system that could think, see, speak, code, and create in ways that mirrored human intelligence. With each generation of AI, he edged closer to that vision. GPT-5 wouldn't get them all the way there, he admitted, but it would take another meaningful step toward a unified, multimodal model.

He imagined a future where you could ask a single question and the AI would decide how best to answer. It might reason through the problem deeply, run background research, write just-in-time code for a bespoke application, or even generate a live, interactive video. That kind of fluid response—shifting effortlessly between thinking, building, and presenting—would be transformative.

To Sam, this wasn't just a technical upgrade. It was the birth of a new interface—one where AI became the bridge between thought and action. A model that didn't just reply to prompts, but that could generate fully formed experiences on demand. A system with perfect video, perfect code, deep logic, and adaptability.

AI already did a little of this, in fragments. But when it could combine everything—vision, language, reasoning, coding—into a single, seamless entity, then something truly powerful would emerge. Sam saw it coming, slowly but surely. It wouldn't arrive all at once. But it would arrive. And when it did, it would change how people interacted with information, creativity, and the digital world forever.

The Meaning of It All

Sam Altman had spent his life chasing questions, not answers. A simple but seismic one eventually emerged in his life: What do you think is the meaning of all this work? The question echoed across decades of effort, across the entire arc of human progress. A

He didn't claim to hold the truth. It was a question for Artificial General Intelligence—AGI—the very thing he was helping humanity build.

Sam didn't see the invention of AGI as the product of a small team locked away in Silicon Valley. He saw it as the culmination of centuries—no, millennia—of human effort. From the early whispers of thought in ancient caves to the first spark of reason that led to the transistor, to the endless iterations of code and silicon, this moment was not sudden. It was inevitable.

He thought about the transistor, discovered in the 1940s. Could those inventors have imagined where their work would lead? The cascading brilliance that followed—millions of engineers, physicists, visionaries—each building on the foundations of those who came before. The story of AI was not about one company or one man. It was about all of us. "This is the output of all of us," he said. And there was a kind of reverence in that.

Before the transistor, there were a hundred billion lives lived. People who laughed, loved, struggled, and sometimes hurt each other. All of them contributed to the ongoing narrative that led to that moment in time. Before those people, there were organisms, bacteria, single-celled life, inching forward on a timeline that was, in his words, "one exponential curve." That, to him, was beautiful. It meant something.

He wondered aloud how many others might be out there—other civilizations, other timelines, other exponential curves. That question, he said, would be the first he would ask an AGI: Are we alone? And he wasn't sure which answer he feared more—yes or no.

It wasn't just philosophy. For Sam, these questions were embedded in the work itself. The mission of OpenAI, the work with his colleagues like Ilya Sutskever and Greg Brockman, wasn't just technical; it was existential. These were people he respected deeply. "They're really good people," he said with warmth. They weren't building toys or tools. They were building the scaffolding of a new era. And they knew it.

The approach they took—iterative deployment and iterative discovery—had its critics. Many believed AGI needed tighter control or slower pacing. Sam understood the concern. But he believed that learning while building, adjusting while progressing, was the only way to meet the moment responsibly. The challenges were hard. The risks were real. But so was the opportunity.

As capabilities advanced, Sam remained hopeful that new tools would emerge just as fast to help with safety, alignment, and ethics. The "capital S" safety problem, as he called it, wasn't an afterthought. It was central to everything. He didn't believe humans could afford to separate progress from responsibility. They had to walk side by side.

"We're going to try our hardest to get to a good place."

Sam Altman saw himself as a steward of something much bigger than any company, any headline, or any title. The meaning of life, for him, wasn't a sentence. It was a movement. It was the slow accumulation of love, pain, ideas, failures, dreams, and atoms—shaping what humanity could be.

He saw the trajectory not as a straight line, but a spiral, winding through biology, technology, philosophy, and wonder. And in that spiral, he found not just progress, but purpose.

He remembered Alan Turing, a man who helped launch this exponential curve. Turing once said that the thinking machine would eventually outstrip human power—and might take control. But for Sam, the control was about understanding rather than domination. He wanted to help humanity become more itself, not less.

The Operating System of Everything

By 2024, Sam Altman had watched ChatGPT evolve into something far greater than a chatbot. What began as a research tool and experimental interface was slowly becoming, in his words, "the operating system for people's lives." It was no longer just something users opened in a browser—it was becoming the interface to their calendars, documents, codebases, personal histories, workflows, and even their thoughts.

At Y Combinator, Sam and his team had already been using agent infrastructure internally. They were interacting with models not just as assistants, but as collaborators, operators, and executors of core processes. And they weren't alone. More and more users were integrating ChatGPT into their personal and professional systems, syncing it with data sources, APIs, and daily routines.

It wasn't just about conversations anymore. It was about persistence—memory, context, continuity. With a model that could run continuously, remember your preferences, and access your tools and documents, you suddenly had something unprecedented. Add to that the arrival of AI-enhanced devices—voice interfaces, wearable agents, smarter browsers—and the AI system became a true extension of your cognitive and digital self.

Sam saw the power in blending memory, real-time data access, and models that could adapt and respond across sessions. Whether that intelligence lived on the cloud or ran locally was a fluid question. Most likely, it would be both. He imagined a hybrid future where heavy tasks happened in OpenAI's massive infrastructure—likely to become the largest in the world soon—and lightweight reasoning happened right on your phone or laptop.

That wasn't just convenient. It was necessary. ChatGPT's growth had been staggering. A mere two and a half years after launch, it had become the fifth most visited website in the world. And if current trends continued, Sam believed it would eventually become the first. But that kind of scale came at a price—compute. The demand was relentless.

Running models of this scale was resource-intensive, costly, and increasingly complex. Compute scarcity had become one of the industry's tightest bottlenecks. "If we could offload even half the ChatGPT workload onto local devices," he admitted, "no one would be happier than us."

Yet, despite the scale, the vision remained grounded. Sam wasn't just chasing growth or domination—he was pushing toward a future where AI was ambient, contextual, helpful. A tool that wasn't just smart, but aligned. Not just powerful, but personal. And the closer OpenAI came to integrating reasoning, memory, local context, and universal access, the closer it came to building not just a product—but a partner. Something that knew you, grew with you, and stayed with you.

The surprise wasn't just how fast it happened—but how natural it had started to feel. And to Sam Altman, that meant they were on the right track.

The Trouble with Advice

When asked to give advice to young people—those in high school or college wondering how to build a meaningful life—Sam Altman never offered a polished answer. He didn't pretend to hold a master key to life's challenges.

Instead, he hesitated, then admitted something unexpected.

"I mostly got what I wanted by ignoring advice."

It was the kind of response that startled people, especially those who came expecting to hear a golden formula. After all, Sam was the president of Y Combinator, co-founder of OpenAI, and a widely admired figure in tech. He had written a blog post titled How to Be Successful that circulated like gospel among aspiring entrepreneurs. It included principles like: compound yourself, believe in yourself almost too much, get good at sales, take risks, build a strong network, and work really hard. It was, by all accounts, solid advice.

And yet here he was, telling young people not to lean on advice too heavily.

To Sam, the problem wasn't that advice was wrong. It was that advice was personal. What had worked for him—his unique path, shaped by personality, luck, curiosity, and ambition—might not work for someone else. In fact, it might distract them from discovering their own way.

He wasn't trying to be contrarian, just honest. There was a real danger, he believed, in outsourcing your choices to the opinions of others. It was tempting to copy the paths of successful people. But doing that too rigidly could rob a person of the messy, unpredictable process of self-discovery.

That processoften didn't feel introspective or wise. "I wish it were that," he said. "It's a lot of just, you know, what will bring me joy, what will bring me fulfillment?" It wasn't that he didn't think about impact or purpose—he did. But those thoughts were often grounded in ordinary, very human questions:

Who do I want to spend my time with?
What kind of work excites me?
What makes me feel useful?

To Sam, the inner compass mattered more than any roadmap someone else could draw. He wasn't suggesting a careless drift through life, but many decisions didn't feel like monumental turning points. They felt natural. Like being a fish in water, just swimming with the current. "That's certainly what it feels like," he said. "I think that's what most people would say if they were really honest about it."

There was something freeing about that. It meant you didn't need to have everything figured out. It meant success wasn't necessarily about following bullet points—it was about following curiosity. Sometimes, that led to coding in a basement. Other times, it meant taking a job that seemed unrelated but ended up sparking a lifelong passion. Sam knew that chasing joy and usefulness often led people to the right places—even if they didn't look like the "right" places at first.

That mindset wasn't without complications. It raised philosophical questions—like the idea, famously posed by Sam Harris, that free will might be an illusion. Sam didn't shy away from those ideas. In fact, he acknowledged them with quiet seriousness. Life could feel predetermined. Choices might be shaped by genetics, environment, even randomness. But that didn't stop him from believing in the value of effort, ambition, and reflection.

He returned often to one idea: alignment. Not just alignment between AI systems and human goals, but internal alignment—between what you do and who you are. He believed that the people who thrived long-term were not just those who "worked hard" but those who found a rhythm that matched their nature. Not hustle for hustle's sake. Not conformity. But authenticity.

Sam's own success came from a mix of traits: high tolerance for risk, obsessive curiosity, and a fierce belief in the future. He encouraged young people to experiment until they found what sparked those same things in them. Take bold risks, yes—but also give yourself permission to change direction. Learn to think independently, not just mimic.

He did believe in ambition, but not the kind of ambition built on status or money. He spoke often about internal drive—doing things not because others expect you to, but because you feel compelled. "Be internally driven," he wrote in that blog post. And in his conversations, it became clear that this wasn't just advice. It was the core of how he lived.

He didn't dismiss strategy. In fact, he saw the value of mastering skills that often got overlooked. Sales, for example. "Get good at sales," he'd say. Not just to sell a product—but to sell an idea, a vision, a company. And networking wasn't just a business tactic—it was about building real, long-term relationships with people you respected. The kind of network that didn't just open doors but built something meaningful with you.

But none of that, he insisted, was worth much if it didn't make you proud of your life.

That was the final part of the question he'd been asked: not just how to build a successful career, but how to build a life you could be proud of. He didn't claim to have all the answers. He just believed the answers were within reach if you stopped trying to live someone else's story.

So what would Sam Altman tell a 17-year-old sitting in a classroom, or a 22-year-old deciding what to do after college?

He might say: Work hard, but not at anything. Work hard at what brings you alive.

He might say: Be bold, not reckless. Take risks that reflect what matters to you.

He might say: Build things. Try. Fail. Get back up. And don't wait for someone to give you permission.

But above all, he'd say: Listen to your own life.

Because no matter how successful someone else looks, no advice will ever be better than learning to trust yourself.

Looking Forward

When Sam Altman spoke about the future, he did so not with bombast, but with quiet awe. For someone at the forefront of artificial intelligence, his sense of wonder remained intact. The unknown didn't intimidate him—it energized him. And the further that future stretched, the more curious he became.

One of the conversations that captured his imagination most was not with a person, but with a machine. Sam was often asked what he looked forward to in the age of AGI—Artificial General Intelligence. His answer was simple: "Please explain to me how all of physics works." He wasn't joking. He wanted a theory of everything. Not a patchwork of equations and approximations, but a complete, unified understanding of the universe. He longed for an AGI smart enough to solve every mystery that had eluded humanity: faster-than-light travel, the nature of consciousness, the solution to NP-hard problems. He didn't just want intelligence—he wanted enlightenment.

But his excitement wasn't purely scientific. He wanted to know if we were alone. He hoped that a future AGI might help us detect extraterrestrial life—not necessarily by discovering it directly, but by guiding humanity toward better tools, smarter experiments, and clearer data analysis. "Maybe it's already in the data," he mused. Maybe we just hadn't seen it yet.

He imagined an AGI that could read the subtle fingerprints hidden in the radio silence of the cosmos, one that could write the blueprint for a better space probe, or suggest a decades-long experiment to uncover what no human could discover alone. It might not bring certainty. But it could bring us closer.

And what if it did discover aliens? What if it whispered that they were already here?

Sam's answer was disarmingly calm. "I think I would just go about my life." His happiness, he explained, didn't hinge on answers or revelations. It came from people—from friends, relationships, meaningful work. An alien revelation wouldn't change the fact that joy was human. Unless, of course, that revelation came with danger. "That threat would have to be, like, literally a fire," he said. Unless it forced an immediate response, he'd likely keep building, keep thinking, keep living.

He wasn't oblivious to how fast things were changing. In fact, he admitted that the pace of digital intelligence had outstripped his own expectations. If someone had told him in 2020 that by 2023, he'd be living in a world shaped by models like GPT-4, he would've expected the world to feel more different than it did. "Probably," he said when asked if it surprised him. But he also pointed to a messy truth: multiple trajectories were playing out at once.

Yes, AI was accelerating. But society? That was murkier. He found it strange—and disappointing—that the same world capable of developing mind-bending tools struggled to respond cohesively to a global pandemic. He expected more unity, more clarity. What he saw instead was division, confusion, and a world whose technological brilliance sometimes only highlighted its social dysfunction.

The contrast puzzled him. "The more technological advancement there is, the more we're going to be having fun with social division," he said, only half-joking. Or maybe, he wondered, the progress didn't create the fractures—it just revealed them. That thought stayed with him. For all our intelligence, we still struggled with basic questions: How far have we really come? How do we discover truth? How do we agree on what matters?

Still, for all his concerns, Sam saw reasons for hope. "When I open Wikipedia, I'm happy," he said. It might seem like a small detail, but to him, it wasn't. Wikipedia was proof that humans could build something extraordinary together. It was flawed, yes. It carried biases, yes. But it was also a triumph—a global act of collective intelligence.

He felt the same way about Google Search. The early 2000s version of the internet—messy, open-ended, full of discovery—had left an imprint on him. It was magical, and its core technologies still amazed him. Now, with GPT, he sensed something even bigger emerging. A new interface to knowledge. A tool that could do what search and encyclopedias had done—only more fluid, more direct. You could have a conversation with it. You could ask questions, and it would ask back.

For Sam, that conversational layer was everything. It meant that people didn't have to be experts to access complex knowledge. They just had to be curious. That shift—where AI moved from search engine to dialog partner—was profound. It brought the wisdom of the world into the intimacy of conversation.

But he also knew that power had consequences. Just as AGI could be a source of discovery and inspiration, it could also destabilize. The future wasn't just bright or dark. It was complex.

He worried about safety. He talked often about the "capital S" safety problem—the need to align advanced systems with human values before those systems became uncontrollable. That concern wasn't theoretical for him. It was central to his work at OpenAI. It guided their iterative approach: move forward carefully, release cautiously, listen constantly. Progress, yes—but paired with reflection.

Sam didn't think the world was ready to slow down. But he hoped it could learn to be deliberate. And that was part of what made his view of the future so compelling. He wasn't utopian. He didn't believe AI would fix everything. Nor was he dystopian. He didn't believe it would destroy everything. He believed the future would be what people made of it. The tools would get better. The questions would get harder. And humans—flawed, beautiful, divided humans—would have to decide what to do with them.

In the end, Sam Altman was less interested in the predictions and more interested in the process. He wanted AGI not because he believed it would answer every question, but because it would let humanity ask better ones. Faster ones. Deeper ones. He wanted to stand on the edge of the known world and keep walking.

And when he reached the limit of human knowledge, he wanted something—or someone—there beside him, ready to ask, "What if?"

That was his vision of the future. Not a timeline. Not a product. But a conversation—ongoing, messy, full of wonder. And in that conversation, perhaps, he found the clearest answer of all.

The Humanoid Frontier

Sam Altman had always believed in sequencing ambition. First, perfect the intelligence—then, give it a body. That had been OpenAI's internal strategy for years: build the brain before building the limbs. But as the cognitive capabilities of models approached a tipping point, Sam could sense the time for robotics was drawing near. Not abstract robotics or simulations—but real robots, operating in the real world.

He envisioned a future where subscribing to the highest tier of ChatGPT didn't just unlock new digital features—it came with a humanoid robot. It sounded wild, maybe even absurd, but he said it with a straight face. That kind of future, he believed, wasn't science fiction anymore.

The mechanical side of robotics had always been grueling. Engineering a body that could walk, grasp, see, and move fluidly through an unpredictable world was far harder than people assumed. At the same time, the cognitive AI—language, decision-making, planning—had also been a puzzle. Now, Sam felt, both were nearing convergence. A robot that could do useful work—real work—was no longer decades away. It was a few focused years out.

He even entertained thought experiments: what if you could build a million humanoid robots the old-fashioned way? Could they automate the entire global supply chain? Could they drive mining trucks, load shipping containers, run foundries, and build even more robots? The recursive possibilities intrigued him. If robots could make more robots, the scaling curve would be steep—exponential even.

Still, he knew the demand would explode beyond anything the current system could produce. The hunger for embodied AI—intelligent machines that could think and act—would surpass society's capacity to manufacture them. That, to him, was the real challenge ahead. Not whether robots were possible. But whether we could build enough of them to meet the world's imagination.

A Mind in Motion

Sam Altman didn't just want smarter chatbots or faster programmers. He wanted machines that could move. Machines that could act. Machines that could do.

The vision of AGI sitting quietly behind a screen struck him as incomplete. If intelligence was going to transform the world, it needed arms and legs—or something equivalent.

**"It would be kind of depressing if we had AGI,
and the only way to get something done
in the physical world was still to send a human."**

That wasn't a fantasy—it was a future Sam expected. Embodied AI wasn't just likely; it was necessary. The intelligence revolution wouldn't stop at keyboards and screens. It would enter warehouses, kitchens, disaster zones, and elderly care facilities. It would build, clean, carry, repair.

OpenAI wasn't yet building humanoid robots at scale, but the idea of "brains for robots" was very much on Sam's radar. The same systems that learned to write code and summarize books might one day learn to hold a paintbrush, sort recycling, or help someone out of bed. Intelligence was powerful, but it was incomplete without agency.

And physical agency brought new challenges. Safety took on different dimensions when machines could act on the world, not just respond to it. Reliability, perception, mechanical precision—all of it needed to mature before the intelligence in silicon could be trusted with the physical world.

But Sam was undeterred. The moment felt like a "phase change"—a transformation not just in technology, but in society. The digital and physical worlds were blending. And as models became more capable, OpenAI's role was shifting too: from research lab to infrastructure provider for a new kind of civilization.

He didn't expect a smooth path. Misuse, misunderstanding, and resistance were inevitable. There would be pushback from programmers nostalgic for traditional coding, or ethicists worried about robotic autonomy. And rightly so. These weren't toys. They were tools of immense power.

Still, Sam believed the reward was worth the risk. Smarter models meant better collaboration, faster problem-solving, deeper creativity. And embodied AI meant a world where people didn't have to risk their lives mining metals, delivering groceries, or cleaning hazardous sites. Machines could step in—not as threats, but as partners.

Looking ahead, he imagined a world where the most skilled humans didn't work harder—they worked with AI. They spoke to it in plain language. They co-designed, co-wrote, co-built. And when the idea needed to be made real in the world, a robot didn't need a complete rewrite—it already understood.

The future wasn't just about artificial general intelligence. It was about useful intelligence. Responsive, adaptive, embodied. And Sam wanted OpenAI to be there first—not just to win, but to shape that future with care, vision, and humility.

The leap from GPT-4 to GPT-5 wasn't the end. It was a signal. Intelligence had crossed a threshold. And everything—language, labor, learning, even locomotion—was about to change.

OpenAI had once ventured into robotics, but the focus shifted. The company had been small then and needed to prioritize. At the time, robotics felt difficult for all the wrong reasons. The challenges weren't inspiring—they were logistical, limiting, and distracting from OpenAI's core mission.

But Sam had a clear vision: they would return to robotics someday. Not with vague ambition, but with clearer vision and readiness.

When the Tools Think

The lights in the office buzzed low, casting long shadows on the whiteboards still scrawled with equations and half-erased prompts. Sam stood alone by the window, eyes tracing the skyline, but his mind was somewhere else entirely.

He thought about the team—just a few dozen of them in the beginning. Brilliant minds. Restless. Sharp. A kind of controlled chaos that somehow turned into something historic. They had built the core of OpenAI's world-changing models like gamblers betting everything on intuition and sweat. Most people only saw the final output, the magic in the box. But Sam knew better. He knew the names, the late-night arguments, the breakthroughs that started as bugs.

And yet, even that wasn't the whole story.

Sometimes, in moments like this, he'd remember the ones who came long before. The miners who unearthed the silicon. The engineers who cracked the physics of semiconductors. The architects of the internet, the inventors of the first clunky machines that no one believed in at the time. Millions of hands over centuries, setting the stage for a few dozen to light the fuse.

That was the real thriller. Not just the code, not just the launch. But the quiet realization that this wasn't theirs alone. It was society's collective bet—layer upon invisible layer of discovery and failure, all stacking up behind that glowing terminal. And Sam, watching the night fold over the city, knew exactly how lucky they were to have stood on that mountain of scaffolding… and dared to strike a match.

The Scaffolding of Power

Sam Altman often saw technology not as a collection of gadgets, but as a long arc, or a scaffolding that humanity continuously built upon. To him, every generation laid another layer of this structure, making it easier for the next to climb higher. The story of progress, in his eyes, was the story of people discovering more science, building better tools, and enabling individuals to do exponentially more than ever before.

That arc stretched far back. A person born a hundred years ago operated in a world so limited compared to the present, it was difficult to draw a fair comparison. Even further back, someone from a thousand years ago would be nearly unrecognizable in ability and influence. Sam believed the fundamental promise of this progression was that with each layer of new tools, each generation became more capable—each person more powerful.

And yet, something about this moment felt distinct to him. Looking ahead to the next ten years, he believed that the biggest change wouldn't come from any one technology alone, but from a shift in what a single individual—or a small group with strong intent—could accomplish. Coordination costs, which had always slowed progress, would shrink in the face of tools that empowered people to act independently and effectively. The result wouldn't just be a little more productivity, but a different kind of world altogether.

It wasn't about adding new features to life. It was about changing the tempo of what could be built, shared, and improved by individuals. Sam envisioned a future where the quality of what people created for each other—software, tools, services, even companies—would dramatically increase, not just in scale, but in meaning.

This wasn't optimism for optimism's sake. It was structural. As the scaffolding rose, so did the reach of human agency. And Sam Altman believed that the next floor was almost within reach.

The Product Overhang

By early 2024, Sam Altman found himself looking at a strange mismatch. The models were moving faster than anyone could build for them. GPT-4 and its successors, particularly the latest versions like GPT-4o, had taken reasoning to another plane entirely—yet, the products people built with them lagged behind. Not because of lack of talent, not because of hesitation, but because the capabilities of the models had leapt ahead of the collective imagination.

He called it the "product overhang"—the gap between what the models could do and what people had figured out how to make with them. "Even if the models stopped improving today," he often said, "there's still a mountain of innovation left to climb." But, of course, the models weren't standing still. They were improving by the week.

Just days ago, GPT-4o had cost five times what it did today. That drop in price wasn't a temporary fluke. It was a glimpse of the curve ahead. The performance-per-dollar equation was collapsing fast, and with it came a massive unlock: the ability for more companies, researchers, and even individuals to build on top of cutting-edge intelligence.

OpenAI, meanwhile, was preparing to release a new open-source model. Sam wouldn't pre-announce it—he wanted the team to enjoy their moment—but he could barely hide his excitement. "People will be astonished," he said. "Much better than they're expecting." He hinted at models that could run locally with near-GPT-4-level power, reshaping what was possible for anyone with a laptop.

But the real frontier, to Sam, wasn't just local inference or falling prices—it was the new square on the periodic table of technology: reasoning models. These weren't just autocomplete machines or fancy text generators. They could plan, reflect, iterate, and even collaborate across sessions. They didn't just respond—they thought.

And yet, very few startups were building with that in mind.

Sam knew why. Most people still thought of AI as a tool to enhance existing workflows: write faster, summarize emails, automate chat. But these models weren't just faster tools—they were a new substrate. The interface between human intention and digital action had fundamentally changed. And in that change, he saw the next generation of billion-dollar companies waiting to be born.

He had seen this pattern before. When smartphones first arrived, people initially just ported desktop apps to smaller screens. It took time before the "mobile-native" wave of products—Uber, Instagram, WhatsApp—realized what phones uniquely enabled. He believed the same was now true for AI. Most products today were "desktop thinking" in an "AI-native" world.

But that tide was starting to turn.

In the last month alone, he had begun to notice a shift. Startups were finally treating reasoning as the center of gravity. They were building interaction models that assumed the AI could carry memory, make plans, hold context over time. They weren't asking "How do I automate this task?" They were asking "What if this entire workflow didn't need to exist in the first place?"

To Sam, that shift was seismic.

The greatest surprise, perhaps, wasn't just the speed of improvement—it was the latency of human adaptation. The models were running; people were still catching up. But that gap was also the opportunity. "This is the best moment to start a company in AI," he'd say to anyone who asked. "You're working with materials no one's built with before. It's like discovering a new element, and you get to invent the chemistry from scratch."

So, he waited—watching, advising, nudging—while the next generation of builders woke up to the power in their hands.

Where the Future Begins

It felt like standing on the edge of a blade—razor-thin, shimmering with promise and risk. Sam Altman often described it that way: the thin edge of the spear. The work he and his team were doing wasn't just about building software or pushing code—it was about placing tools into the hands of millions before most people had even realized what those tools could become. And there was something exhilarating, almost intoxicating, about living there—on the frontlines of the future.

His time at Y Combinator had trained him for this life. Back then, it had been a thrill to walk the halls and recognize the spark in young founders' eyes—the glint of people who were seeing just a little further than the rest of the world. That same energy pulsed through OpenAI. The difference now was scale. They weren't just backing scrappy startups—they were shaping the very frame of civilization's next chapter.

Sure, AI had gone mainstream. Everyone had heard of ChatGPT. But most folks still thought of it as a chatbot—useful for drafting emails or summarizing a memo. They hadn't yet grasped the depth of the iceberg, the world of real intelligence just beneath the surface. Sam knew what was coming: agents that reason, tools that think, systems that build. And they were close.

To live in that sliver of time—just ahead of the wave—was both a burden and a gift. It meant shouldering the responsibility to shape wisely. But it also meant seeing tomorrow a little sooner than the rest. And that, Sam thought, was a hell of a place to live.

The People Equation

Sam Altman knew that breakthroughs didn't come from vision alone—they came from people. Not just any people, but a very specific kind. The kind who burned bright with curiosity, carried the weight of their ambition lightly, and could build—not alone in a vacuum—but together, as a force.

When asked what made OpenAI run, he didn't point to infrastructure or strategy or even code. He pointed to the humans behind it. The first 90% of success, he often said, came down to one thing: hiring really smart people who were also really driven and could function in a team. That was it. No fancy algorithms, no mystical formulas—just people who were motivated, disciplined, and aligned.

What baffled him, though, was how many companies got distracted by everything else. They obsessed over credentials or optics, hiring for pedigree instead of power. Sam ignored the noise. He looked for a different signal: the quiet confidence of someone who had built things that mattered, who didn't wait to be told what to do, who lit up when faced with a hard problem. Someone who, above all else, could play well with others while marching toward the same mountain.

Yes, intelligence mattered. But intelligence without drive, or drive without humility—those were dead ends. The OpenAI team wasn't built for ego; it was built for ambition tempered by alignment. A shared vision. A shared grind.

That formula worked. Time and again, he saw it: teams made up of these kinds of people moved fast, solved problems, and stayed resilient when it counted. In a world racing to define the future of intelligence itself, that clarity—of who to trust in the trenches—was everything.